[Middletons Aberdeen Ltd.

BARNHAM MILL

The Wayfarer's Book) (Frontispiece

The Rambler's
Countryside Companion

The Rambler's
Countryside Companion

A Facsimile Edition of a 1930's book, originally published as

The Wayfarer's Book

by

E. MANSELL

Bounty
Books

A facsimile edition of *The Wayfarer's Book*, the blank pages following full page images are as in the original. The information provided in this book is as recommended and published in 1952. The Publishers shall have no liability with respect to any harm, loss or damage, caused by, or alleged to be caused by, or in any way arising from, or alleged to be arising from information contained in this book. It is not an instruction manual and is presented as general information and should not be considered as a replacement for qualified and professional advice.

First published in Great Britain by Ward Lock & Co., Limited
This edition first published in Great Britain in 2010 by Bounty
Books, a division of Octopus Publishing Group Ltd,
Endeavour House
189 Shaftesbury Avenue
London WC2H 8JY

An Hachette UK Company
www.hachette.co.uk

A CIP catalogue record for this book is available from the
British Library.

ISBN: 978-0-753719-74-9

Printed and bound in China

CONTENTS

FOREWORD

Some years ago, I was asked by a member of a Rambling Club to which I belonged, what was the meaning of the word Lychgate. Not being able to give an explanation, I took the first opportunity of looking into the matter.

From that day I have made it my duty and pleasure to keep a log of everything of unusual interest discovered during my many wanderings.

This little book is the result, and is exactly what the title proclaims it—"*The Wayfarer's Book*"—a collection of scraps and oddments of unusual and extremely interesting facts and information gleaned from all manner of places.

It is designed to help in a small way those hundreds who wish to know still more of the many interesting objects met with during their rambles and to add still further enjoyment to their wanderings.

E. MANSELL.

CHAPTER I

RELICS FROM THE PAST

MEGALITHIC REMAINS

There's much can be learnt of the Men of Old,
  Not only by scholars and sages,
If Wayfarers would their Dolmens behold,
Learn the secrets their High Stones and Barrows unfold,
Trace the Lays of the Ancients—those pioneers bold,
  Not rely on historical pages.

F. HUNT.

To many of us nothing is more interesting than the story of
our predecessors. We love to lift the pall of oblivion and
behold, even in glimpses, the wonders and the splendours
of vanished civilisations. To those who take the time and
trouble to explore, there is rich reward to be found in the
ancient landmarks of our countryside, whether it be the
ruins of a once proud fortification, or a stone monument
marking the place where some ancient chieftain of the past
was buried, or the relics of a temple where once these
prehistoric men worshipped God according to their light.

Menhirs, Dolmens and Cromlechs

Often, when you have been wandering through the
countryside, you must have come across some curious
arrangement of stones, or some earthwork obviously not of
Nature's formation. You may have said to yourself, " I
wonder what that is ? " and gone on your way dissatisfied
because you could not answer your own question.

There are many hundreds of such relics, more or less in a
state of decay, scattered throughout the British Isles, and in

A MENHIR.

this chapter I propose to tell you something of what archæologists know of them. Dates cannot be given with any accuracy, but all these remains are prehistoric and, therefore, many thousands of years old.

The ancient stone structures have been roughly divided into three classes, namely : "Menhirs," "Dolmens" and "Cromlechs." The simplest and most widespread is the menhir, or high stone (from Celtic *maen*, a stone, and *hir*, high). Menhirs occur either alone or in association with other prehistoric remains, and are often of enormous size. The exact purpose of these great upright stones is not known ; but it is supposed that they were erected in connection with a religious cult or to commemorate some great event, or as monuments of famous tribal chieftains.

The idea of setting a stone on end in the gound has occurred to people in all parts of the world from the earliest times, and it persists to-day in the form of obelisks, monuments and tombstones. Imposing as they are in isolation, these enormous stones are far more awe-inspiring when arranged in long rows, as they are in several places in south-western England and elsewhere. A single line of menhirs is known as an alignment. Dual, triple or multiple rows are usually termed " avenues," to distinguish them from the single lines.

A DOLMEN.

BOWL.

The fact that prehistoric men should have moved these huge stones to the chosen spot and then have erected them to form these megalithic structures with nothing but their own strength and possibly a lever to assist them, indicates a relatively high condition of civilisation, for it must have needed some sort of organised rule to bring the tribe together, and some great impulse to make them willing to undertake such a vast work as the erecting of these great stones.

From the menhir we will turn to the next form of megalithic monument, the dolmen (from Celtic *daul*, a table and *maen*, a stone). In their simplest form dolmens consist of three or more stones fixed upright in the ground, on the top of which another, often of great size, is laid flat so as to form a roof. Dolmens were erected as burial chambers, the bodies, often cremated, were deposited within, and the whole covered by a mound of earth, the removal of which in later times has once again left the great stone tables exposed.

These megalithic tombs are especially abundant in Cornwall, Ireland and Wales, but they also occur in many other parts of the British Isles. A notable example is the one known as " Kit's Coty House," near Ashford in Kent.

The term " Cromlech " signifies a stone circle, or ring of standing stones (from Celtic, *crom*, a circle, and *llech*, a

BELL.

DISC.

stone), but having in the past been used to denote dolmens and other objects, the name is sometimes rather misleading. Round these cromlechs popular myth and legends have accumulated to form tales of deeds wrought by the devil, of ogres and dwarfs, of Sabbath-breakers and infidels turned to stone. Such legends often invest these venerable structures with a mystery which deepens their charm.

Cromlechs vary in diameter (one hundred feet is not an uncommon measurement), and are formed of stones of different height—very often they are quite small. In some cases these circles enclose burial mounds, while in others they are connected with one or two avenues. The largest example of this kind of monument is the collection of stones at Avebury in Wiltshire. Far more widely known, however, than the Avebury relic, although considerably smaller in size and of a later date, is Stonehenge, on Salisbury Plain. Undoubtedly, this is one of the most remarkable Megalithic monuments in the world, for although the great structure has suffered considerably with the passage of years, enough remains to enable us to realise its pristine grandeur.

While studying these monuments, many other terms will be met with, such as "Trilithon," "Sarsen," "Barrows," etc.

"Trilithon" is the name given to a structure composed of two menhirs with a lintel across their tops. Several perfect examples of this form are still to be seen at Stonehenge.

Sarsen Stones

Throughout the south and south-east of England, where there are chalk hills, sarsen stones are fairly common. These large stones are relics of the Eocene age. This was the geological age when southern England was covered by a great sheet of fine sand and gravel which has been gradually swept away by wind and rain, leaving behind only the harder portions which had been naturally concreted together by siliceous cement. These hardened cores are the sarsen stones. The name Sarsen has an interesting derivation. It is a corruption of the word " Saracen," a name applied by early writers first to the Mohammedans of Syria, and at a later date to pagans generally, and even to giants ; and as folk-lore tales usually connect all stone circles and megalithic monuments with the work of heathens and devils, one can readily understand that any stone of uncommon size or outline soon became a Saracen or heathen stone, which the Wiltshire tongue has shortened in due time to Sarsen.

The country folk, always picturesquely minded, often refer to them as " Grey Wethers," as from the distance they have the appearance of a flock of titanic sheep reclining at ease upon the pasturage of the Downs.

ANCIENT BURIAL MOUNDS

Barrows

Barrow is the name given to the burial mounds of the Neolithic and Bronze Ages and they are of more elaborate plan than the dolmen. (The word comes from the Anglo-Saxon, *beorg*, a hill or hillock.) These ancient mounds can be roughly divided into two classes : the Long Barrow and the Round Barrow, with its three variants, the Bowl, the Bell and Disc Barrow.

Long Barrow. This is the older form and is characteristic of the Neolithic age. Some of the long barrows are only mounds of earth, while others have an interior chamber of stone approached by a stone-lined passage. These burial mounds are roughly egg-shaped in plan and vary from two to four hundred feet in length. They lie usually with the long axis east and west, the chamber and entrance both being at the higher or eastern end. It is the construction of this chamber, with large stones, which marks them as megalithic structures. The earth of which they are composed was dug out from a trench on either side of the mound. This trench did not, however, continue round the two ends of the barrow. No metal objects have been discovered in long barrows, though leaf-shaped flint arrow-heads have been found and occasionally rough hand-made pottery.

The long barrow, probably a family or tribal burial ground, was sometimes surrounded by a low wall of dry masonry. Both ordinary burials and cremation (in some restricted localities) were practised by Neolithic men, and in many cases where the body was buried unburnt, the bones are often more or less disjointed, as if the skeleton had been placed in the mound after the flesh had decayed.

It is a curious fact that the skulls found in the long barrows of Britain are uniformly long-headed, while those in the round barrows are of round-headed people. Compared with the round barrows, the long barrows are comparatively rare, those in North Wiltshire and Gloucestershire being the best examples of the chambered type, the unchambered occurring chiefly in South Wiltshire, Dorset, Westmorland and Yorkshire.

Round Barrow. The round barrows raised over their dead by the men of the Bronze Age, are, as already stated, far more numerous and more widely-distributed than the Neolithic long barrows. They usually occur in groups and vary considerably in diameter and height.

It is now believed that the three forms of round barrows were in use at one and the same time, but that the Bowl Barrow was the earliest, followed by the Bell, and that the Disc is the latest form of all.

The "Bowl Barrow" is like an inverted bowl and is, perhaps, more frequently encountered than the others. It is, however, considerably smaller in diameter than the other types. The "Bell" type reaches its highest development around Stonehenge, and unlike the long barrow is entirely surrounded by a circular ditch, from which the earth for the mound was excavated; within the circular ditch is a level area of turf, from the centre of which rises the mound in a graceful conical form, five to fifteen feet in height. The diameter of these Bell Barrows is often upwards of one hundred feet, so that the structure is considerably more impressive than the Bowl Barrow.

The "Disc Barrow" was so named by Dr. Thurnam, the great barrow expert. These barrows consist of a circular area, level with the surrounding turf. This area is enclosed by a bank with a ditch on the inside, both usually very regular and well constructed. In the centre of the circle is a mound rarely more than a foot high containing the remains of the dead.

As a rule, the body was buried in a hole in the ground, and this grave was covered with the mound. In some cases other interments were made in the mound. Stone cists were sometimes used for burial purposes in the opening phase of the Bronze Age, but later they became rare, and the sepulchral structures erected were built of smaller blocks than those used by Neolithic men.

The "finds" in round barrows include, besides pottery and stone arrow-heads, weapons of bronze and occasionally ornaments of gold and amber.

Although the men who built these barrows have been called Bronze Age people, it does not follow that their

LONG BARROW.

weapons were made exclusively of that metal, for in all ages there is a perceptible overlap from the former culture.

The term "Cairn," used in Scotland to indicate a barrow, is from Gaelic *carn*, a heap. Tumulus (Lat. *tumulus*, a mound, pl. *tumuli*) is another name by which a barrow is sometimes known.

ANCIENT TRACKWAYS AND MARK STONES

There are other large stones met with about the country-side that do not come under the headings already mentioned. Some, such as Mark Stones, are the work of prehistoric men, others are the work of Nature.*

Mark Stones take us back to a time long before the dawn of history, when there were few settlements or villages, and man more often dwelt in caves or hut hollows. At that time his wants were few, for he lived principally by hunting

* See Perched Blocks, Chapter VI.

and made most of his necessities at home. But few as his requirements were, he could not always find the raw material in his own neighbourhood. Salt for instance, useful for preserving his meat, was in most districts only obtainable from a distance. The same condition applied to his cutting implements, flint flakes ; these he could secure only from the chalk districts, and he was often compelled to make a journey of many miles through wild country to obtain them. But without them he could not make his hunting weapons and knives, and lacking these, he could never have survived ; therefore he was obliged to fetch them from the distant places where they were obtainable. This meant that hunters and others had often to cross unknown territories in search of supplies, and as in those far off days no estab- lished roads existed, they had perforce to lay out trackways to enable them to find their way. Most of the evidence we possess shows that the people of these remote ages were at peace with one another and that fighting times only came to our island with later foreign invasions. These peaceful conditions enabled primitive man to make a bee-line to reach the distant supply spots as there was not the necessity of long detours to avoid hostile tribes.

To-day it is possible to obtain only fragmentary evidence of the routes taken by some of these early trackways. The tracks of the Middle Ages may be traced with a certain degree of accuracy, but the ways by which the first settlers of our island moved have undergone many changes and much obliteration.

As has already been pointed out, these very early track- ways of Britain invariably ran straight across the country, up and down, from hill-top to valley, from settlement to settlement.

It will undoubtedly puzzle many wayfarers that in an age long before any form of instrument, scientific or rudi- mentary, was known to man, such accurate alignment was attained over long distances. The method employed was that of marking out the trackways with stones known as " Mark Stones." The alignment of these stones was arrived at in the same way as one obtains alignment of the sights on a rifle, only, in the case of the ancient track makers, two staves were probably used. A typical Mark Stone is either unworked or only very slightly worked, or " pecked " into shape. They are of many forms, except, perhaps, flat upright slabs, and usually have some appearance differing from chance stones in the district. Often they are of non-local stone. They vary from one or two feet to twenty feet in height.

The Wayfarer may ask : " How is all this known ? " It is known because the stones, in a number of instances, exist to this day and can be seen in many rural districts. In some villages more than one may be found. It is not always discovered in its original state, for when Britain embraced Christianity, many of these pagan Mark Stones were converted into Christian Crosses, either by utilising the stone as the base and erecting a shaft on it, or, if it was already an upright stone, by having a Cross cut on it.

MARK STONE.

The churchyard cross at Vowchurch, Herefordshire, is an example of a Cross built on to a Mark Stone. Another churchyard Cross in the same county, that at Bosbury, when moved from its original site in 1796, was discovered to have a large Mark Stone embedded in its fabric.

Mark Stones, especially when placed at a point where two or more trackways crossed, often became haunts where trading took place during these early days. Many of these old track crossings are still crossroads to-day, and although the tracks themselves have changed out of all recognition, the ancient Mark Stone which marked the crossing is still often to be seen there, as at Pembridge, where the old stone has been used to support an oak pillow, the socket-stone of the fourteenth century Market Cross.

Origin of Place Names

Old trackways and Mark Stones can often be traced if the origin of place names is studied. In some instances it will be found that the names of towns, villages and farms obviously have no connection with any characteristic of the place itself, with the people who live there, or with the occupation they follow at the present time, but have, in all probability, been derived from some feature or incident associated with the place many hundreds, sometimes thousands of years ago.

Place names having the prefix " Chip," " Chap," or " Cheap," as Chipstead, Chipping Norton, Chipping Campden and Chippenham, are all probably situated on some ancient flint track, or were connected in some way with the flint trade, the name being an onomatopoetic one describing the sound of knocking off flakes of flint.

Chapman was the name given to the early flint traders, and the name Chapman's Sands, Chapman's Ford, and the fine Chapman Barrows, one hundred and fifty feet up on Exmoor, all undoubtedly derived their name from these early flint men.

Such names as Knapper's Farm, Flinty Knapp and Knapper's Barton also have some connection with the ancient flint trade. They were probably trading spots, for the man who chips flints is still known as a flint knapper.

The old salt, pottery and various other trading tracks can also be traced in the same way.

That " mark," found in scores of place-names, indicated a sighting point on some ancient trackway, is certain ; but it also, in many instances, gave the name to the markets which grew to be held at such stones.

DENE HOLES

Mysterious artificial pits, known as Dene Holes, are to be found in various parts of the chalk districts of southern England, but chiefly in Kent and Essex, along the lower banks of the Thames. They are often popularly attributed to the Danes, but as many of them were undoubtedly excavated centuries before these people arrived in our country, this suggestion can scarcely be correct.

The general construction of dene holes varies but little. The entrance consists of a circular shaft, some three feet in diameter, sunk vertically to any distance from 40 feet to

80 feet, through gravel and other overlaying strata down to the chalk. When the chalk is reached, the shaft opens out into a domed chamber 16 feet to 18 feet high, with a roof of chalk usually 3 feet thick. As a rule, the walls contract slightly as they approach the floor. In a few cases the chamber has been extended into quite a moderate-sized cave, the roof of which is often supported by pillars of chalk which have been left standing. As a general rule, there is one chamber only below each shaft. Where galleries are found connecting the chambers of several dene holes, they are usually the work of a people of a much later period.

The tool work on the walls and shaft of these pits is often carried out with great precision, but that of the roof is frequently uneven, the awkwardness of the position no doubt hampering the miners in their work.

Markings and pick-holes discovered in some of the dene holes show that, in all probability, they were made by bone or horn picks. Many of these picks have been found in Essex and Kent, although very few other relics of archæological value have been discovered in any of the known holes.

In the sides of many of the entrance shafts, horizontal holes or footholds were cut to enable the miners or quarrymen to climb up and down without a ladder, but probably with the aid of a grass rope hanging from a cross beam at the top.

Isolated dene holes have been found, but they usually appear in groups, the most important of which are at Grays Thurrock, in Essex. Others are in the districts of Woolwich, Bexley and Gravesend, while more doubtful specimens occur as far west as Berkshire and Hampshire.

Endless theories have been advanced in connection with these mysterious holes, and much tradition has gathered round them. In some instances it has been suggested that they were excavated as silos, or underground storehouses for grain. Another idea is that they were hiding places or dwellings. A third suggestion is that they were draw-wells for the extraction of chalk for agricultural uses.

Local tradition often connects these holes with smugglers. The theory that the excavations were made in order to get flints for the making of implements is quite impossible, as a careful examination of a few dene holes will show.

Why they are called dene holes, or whence the name comes is not known.

Chapter II

TREASURES FROM OTHER DAYS

SANCTUARY

" If anyone be guilty of death and he flee to a
church, let him have his life and make satisfaction
as the law may direct him. If anyone put his hide
in peril (punishable by stripes) and flee to a church,
be the scourging forgiven him."

INE, King of Wessex, 680 A.D.

In many parts of the country, relics of ancient and long-
discontinued customs are still to be seen by any observant
wayfarer. Sanctuary Knockers, Frith Stools, and Crosses
are, possibly, among the most ancient and interesting.

The idea of sanctuary is of great antiquity, and its origin
is uncertain. Something analogous to it can be traced in
several pagan communities, while among the Jews there
were Cities of Refuge to which a fugitive might flee. Many
ancient temples and altars of Greece and Rome gave protection to criminals ; but the Roman law did not recognise
the use of Christian sanctuaries until towards the end of the
fourth century.

Although probably practised in England in the latter days
of the Roman occupation, it was not until the revival of
Christianity in the sixth century that proof was recorded
of its actual use.

The earliest extant mention of the rights of sanctuary in
England is contained in the code of laws issued by the
Anglo-Saxon King, Ethelbert (King of Kent), in about the
year 600 A.D.

Ine, King of Wessex in 680 A.D., made further laws,
while in 887 A.D., Alfred the Great drew up others, all of
which laid down exact instructions concerning sanctuaries.
Athelstan, Ethelred, Canute, and William the Conqueror

continued the practice, and indeed, up to the time of James I, laws relating to the privilege of sanctuary are to be found.

During the Reformation, sanctuaries suffered drastic curtailment of their privileges and an act of James I, in 1623–4, finally abolished, as far as crime was concerned, all sanctuary throughout the kingdom.

Sanctuary Knockers. The legend of the Sanctuary Knocker, that any poor wretch flying for his life, or from the State's "justice," who grasped the door knocker of the church was considered to have claimed the sanctuary and immunity of the church, seems to be doubted by some eminent authorities, while others accept it in its entirety and even offer proof of their argument by certain historical references.

THE SANCTUARY KNOCKER, DURHAM CATHEDRAL.

Another point in favour of the ideal is that sanctuary frequently commenced in the churchyard, or even at the boundaries of the land owned by a monastery. For example, in Beverley Minster, sanctuary started a mile and a half in either direction from the Minster boundary and gradually increased in power as one approached the high altar and frith stool, to which was attached the greatest possible security. To violate the protection of sanctuary was an offence for which a penalty of from £8 to £144 was inflicted, with the exception of the violation of the frith stool, which was too grave an offence to be compensated by a pecuniary penalty and was only redeemable by the death of the offender.

Concerning the rights of sanctuary at Hexham Priory, an old writer tells us that " by seizing anyone, flying for refuge, within the four crosses on the outside of the town, a penalty of sixteen pounds was incurred ; within the town the penalty was thirty-two pounds ; within the walls of the churchyard forty-eight pounds, within the doors of the choir one hundred and forty-four pounds ; and besides these penalties, penance, as for sacrilege, for each offence ;

but they who shall presume to seize anyone in the stone chair near the altar, called the Frid-stool, or at the shrine of the holy relicks, behind the altar, for such flagitious crime, shall not be allowed to purchase remission by any sum of money, but shall be boot-less, incapable of pardon."

The religious authorities, however, having given their powerful protection to a fugitive, did not actually countenance his crime.

THE FRITH STOOL, BEVERLY MINSTER.

Connected, in England, with the privilege of sanctuary was the practice of abjuration of the realm. By the ancient common law, a person accused of felony might fly for safeguard of his life to sanctuary, and there, within forty days, go, clothed in sackcloth, before the coroner, confess the felony and take an oath of abjuration of the realm, whereby he undertook to quit the realm, and not return without the king's licence. Upon confession, he became attainted of the felony and forfeited all his goods, but had time allowed him to fulfil his oath.

The abjurer started forth on his journey bareheaded and clothed in sackcloth, and, armed only with a wooden cross to indicate the protection of the Church, had to make his

A TYPICAL OLD PREACHING CROSS.

DUNSTER MARKET CROSS.

way to the coast as quickly as possible. He was compelled to keep to the king's highway, and was not allowed to remain more than two nights in any one place.

Frith Stools. Other ancient treasures left to remind us of this deeply-rooted custom are the stone chairs or Frith (Peace) Stools. These are extremely rare, only two such remaining in this country, one at Beverley Minster, which dates from the days of Athelstan (c.900 A.D.), and another at Hexham, which was probably the actual Bishop's chair, the cathedra of the Saxon church, and used as such by St. Wilfrid at the time when he was Bishop of Hexham. It is probably the oldest episcopal and most venerable stone seat in England, possibly in Christendom (c.700 A.D.).

Sanctuary Crosses. These frequently marked the boundaries of lands owned by a monastery and are less common than the knockers. Many of them suffered badly when the civil power of the church was abolished. Perhaps the best example of these romantic crosses is the Sharon Sanctuary Cross, near Ripon, a relic of very early Saxon times, which, with a strip of the adjoining land, has been recently presented to the National Trust to be preserved for all time. To-day, nothing but the base of the cross is left ; but it tells a tale which takes us back to an age when a law of clemency, a ruling of pity and mercy, was considered to be even more fundamental in import than strict justice.

The right of sanctuary was finally abolished by James I in 1624, but in the vicinity of many old cathedrals and churches you will still find the name perpetuated. The thoroughfare, Broad Sanctuary, in Westminster, for instance, is the site of the sanctuary precincts of Westminster Abbey of olden days.

ANCIENT CROSSES

Apart altogether from religious and historical associations, the beauty of structure and design of many of our old crosses make a search for them well worth while. Often broken and battered by storms, damaged by fanatical iconoclasts and neglected by those whom they most concern, these memorials of the past are still to be found in many corners of our country, sometimes situated imposingly at the cross-roads in a busy town, sometimes less prominently in a sheltered by-way of the countryside.

The most ancient and primitive crosses are probably those scattered about the county of Cornwall. They are of a form peculiar to the county, simple, upright stones of granite, round-headed, with a cross worked upon them, either incised or in relief. They are, in effect, tombstones of Romano-British Christians. Most of these rudely-fashioned crosses seem to have been set up by the early missionaries, chiefly from Ireland, who established oratories in this then wild and trackless land and set up these crosses to guide the faithful to them.

The old crosses of our countryside can be roughly divided into various classes. Some are known as *Preaching Crosses*, others as *Market Crosses*. A number of them are classed as *Memorial Crosses*, and were erected in memory of some beloved object or in commemoration of some event of local importance. *Sanctuary* or *Boundary Crosses* are far less common than the others. These crosses frequently marked the boundaries of lands owned by a monastery, and occasionally were erected over the graves of heroes, kings, bishops, etc.

An Old Tithe Barn.

Most of the crosses in our villages are either Preaching Crosses or Market Crosses. They often date back to the seventh and eighth centuries, when Saxon Britain was being Christianised. Many of the earliest and best are to be found in Northumbria and Derbyshire and are noble and vigorous works of art. To enjoy to the full the variety of their quaint carvings, as, for instance, birds and beasts playing hide-and-seek among vine-scrolls and knot work, one must see the crosses themselves.

It will be found that many of the Preachin Crosses were erected near old monasteries or priories, probably by the monks themselves, although historic proof of this is lacking. It will be remembered that the Preaching Friars and Monks did great good among the poor and the outcast. At the same time they aroused much jealousy among the parish priests, who would often forbid them to preach in the churches, or even from the churchyards. The Friars at such times proclaimed their doctrines to the people from the highways and wayside.

Many of these old Crosses are mounted upon a broad flight of steps, which formed an excellent platform and raised the preachers well above their listeners.

As time went on, a number of the Preaching Crosses developed into meeting places of a commercial as well as a religious nature. It is easy to see the reason for this, for what more inviting place could be found on which to display one's basket of eggs, butter and other produce than the steps of the Cross where everyone was wont to gather ? Thus the Preaching Crosses also became definite meeting places for the buying and selling of wares, and were, no doubt, the origin of many now important markets.

This dual use naturally led to many structural alterations and additions. The weather in those days, as far as one can gather, was just as inclement and fickle as to-day, so there soon arose the necessity to provide some shelter for the persons using them for the sale of their wares. The main idea of the Cross still persisted, but a roof was often built around the shaft, leaving the cross to dominate the whole. It is doubtful whether there are two crosses absolutely identical in form and design. Some are examples of slenderness and delicacy of workmanship, while others are outstanding by reason of their massive strength.

As time went on, the crosses began to be connected more and more with the business life of the town or village, and as the need for greater accommodation arose, an upper chamber above the ground floor open stage was often introduced, until we have a great variety of types, ranging from the early simple forms to the elaborately sculptured and ornate Gothic specimens of Salisbury and Chichester.

A careful study of our old crosses is a very fascinating one for those who have a mind for such things ; for there is a wonderful variety of these structures which, no longer useful, remain as a reminder of the long story of our nation's life from early Christian days. In some cases, in the smaller villages, the wayside cross may quite well constitute the main, if not the only feature of note.

TREASURES FROM OTHER DAYS

TITHES AND TITHE BARNS

A group of old barns nestling round a farmstead is always a charming sight, but perhaps the most impressive of them are the ancient tithe barns, many of which still remain, interesting relics of the past life of England. These tithe barns were formerly attached to some monastery or other religious house, and were often built " as strong as a church and as fine as a minster." In them was stored the grain and

MEMORIAL SUNDIAL TO WILLIAM WILLETT, THE ORIGINATOR OF SUMMER-TIME.

other produce that represented the tithes paid by those who farmed the adjacent land, for in those days tithes were paid in kind and not in money.

The first introduction of tithes into England is ascribed to Offa, King of Mercia, at the close of the eighth century. The usage passed into the other kingdoms of Saxon England, and was in the end made general for all the country by Ethelwulf. For centuries tithes were the chief source of revenue for the church and the immensity of these store-houses gives us some idea of how the churches and monasteries acquired their wealth.

The tithes collected from the people of the parish were originally intended for the relief of the poor and for the upkeep of the chancel, and not for the maintenance of the parish priest. The latter was at first merely the collector ; later he was permitted to retain a portion of the amounts to augment his income, which previously came from glebe, free-will offerings and fees.

Tithes were of two kinds, *Rectorial*, or greater ; *Vicarial*, or lesser. The Rectorial tithes consisted of produce from such things as grow out of the earth, as corn, hay, peas and beans. The Vicarial tithes consisted of produce from such things as are nourished on the earth, as sheep and pigs.

All this was prior to 1835-6, when an Act of Parliament was passed by which tithes in kind were commuted into a tithe rent charge, payable in cash in January and July, the charge being based on the average price of corn over seven years. This held good until 1925, when Parliament stabilised tithe as a fixed charge. Since then prices have crashed and tithe paying has become, in some cases, an impossible burden.

The magnificent style and picturesque surroundings of some tithe barns makes them a glory to gaze upon, and they can never fail to arouse the interest of a true wayfarer. Many have a definitely ecclesiastical character, their porches being comparable with the transepts of great churches. Most of the surviving tithe barns are of stone. Nevertheless, there are a few of brick and of weatherboards. The roofs are most generally of slate or stone, as one would expect with stone buildings ; but there are a few thatched tithe barns and tiled examples are fairly common.

SUNDIALS

In no place does a sundial look so well as in some old-world garden, where :

> " Serene he stands among the flowers,
> And only marks life's sunny hours ;
> For him dark days do not exist—
> The brazen-faced old optimist."

GEORGE ALLISON.

It was not until the sixteenth century that sundials became fashionable in private gardens ; but for centuries they have been in existence in many parts of the world. In fact, the sundial is one of the oldest memorials of the past that has survived the rush of modern life. Often they can still be found in the spot where they were originally placed in the days long before any other means of reckoning time had been devised.

This mode of computing time was apparently in use long before the beginning of the Christian era and must have been one of man's first applications of a knowledge of the apparent motion of the sun.

The earliest mention of a sundial has been thought to be that

SUNDIAL ON BEWCASTLE CROSS.

found in the Old Testament (2 Kings, xx, 11) and (Isaiah xxxviii, 8), where the following reference occurs : "Behold, I will bring again the shadow of the degrees, which is gone down in the sundial of Ahaz, ten degrees backwards." The date of these references would be about 710 B.C., but there is no direct proof that there was a sundial.

The oldest of all sundials of which we have any certain knowledge is an |____ shaped Egyptian specimen in the Berlin Museum, in which the upright of the |____ throws longer or shorter shadows along the horizontal limb, which is divided into six hours. In the morning, the upright was turned to the east and in the afternoon to the west.

Another early type was the hemicycle, or hemisphere, of the Chaldean astronomer Berosus, who probably lived about 300 B.C. It consisted of a hollow hemisphere placed with its rim perfectly horizontal and having a style, the point of which was at the centre. So long as the sun remained above the horizon the shadow of the point would fall on the inside of the hemisphere, and the path of the shadow during the day would be approximately a circular arc.

Herodotus recorded that the Greeks derived from the Babylonians the use of the gnomon, but the great progress made by them in geometry enabled them in later times to construct dials of great complexity and ingenuity.

The Romans adopted the sundial from the Samnites, the first being erected at Rome in the year 290 B.C., by Papirius Cursor, who had taken it from them ; but the first dial actually constructed for Rome was made in 164 B.C. by order of Q. Marcius Philippus.

The Arabians attached great importance to gnomonics, the principles of which they had learned from the Greeks ; but they greatly simplified and diversified the Greek constructions.

The various forms of dials are usually named according to their position : *Vertical Dials* when traced on a vertical plane facing one of the cardinal points ; *Horizontal Dials* when on a horizontal plane ; *Equinoctial Dials* when the plane is at right angles to the earth's axis, etc.

In England the oldest dials are often to be seen on the south walls of some old churches, for in spite of decay and rebuilding many of these ancient time-markers have been spared, and are, naturally, of great archæological interest. The simplest of all are the Anglo-Saxon examples, which consist of a few lines radiating from a central hole in which a wooden style could be inserted. In most of these dials the day is divided into four tides of three hours each. One excellent specimen may be seen at Daglingworth, in Gloucestershire. Another example of this type of sundial is on Bewcastle Cross, which dates back to 670 A.D.

During the eighteenth century, clocks and watches began to supersede sundials, and the latter gradually fell into disuse, except in gardens, where they are used more as decorations than timepieces.

With the introduction of Summer Time (it was introduced as a war measure in 1916 and made permanent by Act of Parliament, 1925) most sundials were, of course, one hour slow in their calculations ; but not so the one erected in memory of William Willett, the originator of Summer Time. This sundial, which stands in a beautiful strip of woodland some eighty acres in extent at Pett's Wood, Kent, indicates only correct hours when Summer Time is operative.

Chapter III

MORE TREASURES

DOVECOTES

In recent years there have been pleasing signs of a revival of interest in the ancient dovecotes of our countryside. For too long these architectural reminders of a vanished feature of rural life have been allowed to fall into neglect and even to decay.

So far as is known, dovecotes were first introduced into our island by the Norman Conquerors; but most of the surviving specimens were built in the sixteenth and seventeenth centuries. These picturesque links with the past vary considerably in design and construction, the earliest Norman forms being circular in plan, with the thick walls characteristic of their architecture. Later styles, like the beautiful specimen at Naunton, near Stow-on-the-Wold, are rectangular; others, again, are eight-sided. One of the oldest specimens is at Patcham, near Brighton. This dates from the late fourteenth or early fifteenth century, is circular in shape and built of flint. After the sixteenth century, however,

DOVECOTE ON THE ARROW AT CARDISLAND.

brick seems to have been more generally used, though there are also several fine examples in half-timber style to be seen.

The interior of a cote housed anything from 500 to 4,000 birds in nesting hole apertures built into the thickness of the walls. In some of the cotes a bath was provided for the birds, and a number of the older circular cotes contained a " potence," i.e. a device of a ladder fixed to a wooden frame which revolved round a central pole, by means of which it was possible to reach the upper nests to secure the young birds and eggs.

In the Middle Ages and even later, the right of keeping pigeons and building cotes was a prerogative of " the Lords of the Manor "—a term which embraced ecclesiastical dignitaries. For them the pigeons were both a means of subsistence and a source of increased income. On the other hand, the reservation was a sad injustice to their feudal inferiors, who not only had to submit to seeing their crops raided daily by the numerous birds, but were unable to protect themselves, for the shooting of pigeons was an offence visited with severe penalties, and in certain circumstances was punishable with death.

The extent of the pigeon-cult in this country may be gauged by the statement of Samuel Hartlib, Milton's friend, who records that towards the middle of the seventeenth century the number of English dovecotes was estimated at 26,000.

MARTELLO TOWERS

These curious towers, which are such a prominent feature of our east and south coasts, were built about the year 1804, and were part of a system of coastal defence. At that time, England was troubled about the possibilities of Napoleon invading our shores, and the British Government erected these circular forts to prevent any landing. They were never put to the test, however, as our army kept Napoleon's troops fully engaged elsewhere. Thus the Martello Towers stood not idle, but inactive and the people sang :

When, O when, does this little Boney come ?
P'r'aps he'll come in August, and p'r'aps he'll stay at home.

AN OLD CIRCULAR DOVECOTE.

And if he did come, what then? There are popular songs enough to tell us what would happen; one old Sussex rhyme ran:

If Boneypart
Should have the heart
To land at Pemsey Level,*
Then my three sons
With their three guns
Would blow him to the Devil.

The name " Martello " is a corruption of Martella, the
towers being named after a somewhat similar structure that
stood on Cape Martella in Corsica. This tower was bom-
barded by a British squadron of three ships of the line and
two frigates in September, 1793, when this country was
supporting the Corsican insurgents against the French.
After a short struggle it was captured by a landing party.

Up to that time the tower had provided little to justify
its subsequent reputation. During February of 1794,
however, a fresh assault was made. One thousand, four
hundred troops were landed, and the tower was again
attacked, from both land and sea. For two and a half hours
the cannonade continued, but apparently made no impression
until a hot shot set fire to the bass junk with which, to the
depth of five feet, the immensely thick parapet was lined.
Only then, after a gallant fight, did the garrison surrender,
and, much to the surprise of the attackers, it was discovered
that the only armament the tower boasted consisted of
two 18-pounders and one 6-pounder.

The prolonged resistance offered by these three guns
seems to have led to the conclusion that towers of this
description were specially formidable and would prove a
strong defence against the army of Napoleon.

The height of the towers was between 30 and 40 feet,
with a circumference at the base of well over 100 feet.
The walls were of solid masonry, some six or more feet
thick, and were practically indestructible by the guns of
those days. The magazine was placed at the bottom of
the tower, over which were two vaulted rooms, where the
small garrison of from six to twelve men lived. Many of
these quaint little fortresses were surrounded by a fosse,
40 feet or so wide, across which was a drawbridge. Access
to those without a fosse was gained by means of a ladder,
communicating with a door about 20 feet above the ground.

In most cases the defensive weapons consisted of a swivel

* The modern Pevensey.

38

gun placed on a platform on the flat roof, supplemented by howitzers, for flanking purposes, which fired over a low masonry parapet. The chief defect of the towers seems to have been their weakness against vertical fire.

While the Martello tower owes its reputation and its widespread adoption in Great Britain to a single incident of modern warfare, the round masonry structure entered by a door raised high above the base is to be found in many lands, and is one of the earliest types of masonry fortification.

CROSSING THE STREAM

" Twenty Bridges from Tower to Kew
  Wanted to know what the River knew,
  For they were young and the River was old,
  And this is the tale that the River told."
        RUDYARD KIPLING, " The River's Tale."

One of the earliest problems our early ancestors had to face was that of " Crossing the Stream." Often the waters flowed deep and swift, and formed serious barriers to the journeyings of these primitive folk, when the only method of reaching the other side was to walk or wade across at some shallow place. For many centuries this was the only way of crossing the stream, and for generations the same shallow places were used until eventually they became known by the name of fords.

A MARTELLO TOWER AS IT IS TO-DAY.

There are many present day place-names which serve to remind us of the location of these ancient crossings. There is even some reason to believe that the Thames in London was fordable at low tide before the days of the Romans, when the river was, of course, three times the width that it is to-day and therefore much shallower. It is obvious, however, that many of the other rivers and streams have also undergone considerable changes since the day the ford received its name. Some have become so much deeper as to be unfordable, while others have shrunk from great waterways to mere streams that can be stepped across.

Fords, however, even the best of them, were inclined to be dangerous ; and when the first crude wheeled vehicles came into existence many difficulties must have been met with, particularly " grounding." That is probably why we find, at a later date, the paved ford was invented. This consisted of a carefully arranged stone causeway below the water. There is a very ancient example of this type of ford still to be seen on the River Avon, near Evesham.

Stepping-stones across the stream were in all probability introduced about the same time, and these had the advantage of enabling people to cross without getting wet.

The next improvement in the method of " crossing the stream " was the ferry. When the first ferry was started is, of course, quite impossible to say ; but ferries were in use when the Romans came to Britain, for Bede refers to one at Sarre, on the River Stour, Kent.

No English river of any size is forded now ; but the wayfarer will find many places where some little-used lane becomes submerged where it is crossed by a stream. On the other hand, ferries are still quite common and are in daily use on many of our rivers and streams. Some of the oldest in Britain still working are those used by the Canterbury Pilgrims during their journey from Winchester to Canterbury.

Ferries vary in size and in the means of propulsion. Sometimes they are merely row boats, sometimes rafts drawn across the stream by means of chains. Most of the ferries of the rivers of Norfolk and Suffolk are of this kind. They consist of huge rafts bound with iron. When the river is clear of traffic these drift across on chains. At St. Olaves, there has been a crossing of the River Waveney from time immemorial. In the reign of Edward I a ferry at this place was worked by one Sireck, a fisherman, who carried people over in his boat and received for his services, " bread, herrings and such like things to the value of twenty shillings per year."

But fords and ferries are at best only inadequate substitutes for the bridge. There have been bridges in England for at least two thousand years; we know the Romans built a number, and it is possible, but not certain, that long before the Roman occupation primitive men had had wit enough to make elementary bridges.

There have always been rivers and streams to cross, and these ancient people no doubt devised an easier and quicker means of crossing than by scrambling down one bank and up another. One day some savage of genius placed a big

A CLAPPER BRIDGE, NEAR POSTBRIDGE, DARTMOOR.

slab of stone, with the help of his fellow tribesmen, from bank to bank of a stream, and formed the first man-made bridge. You can see such a bridge in the Wycollar Valley, Lancashire.

The bridge known as the Weaver's, in the same valley, is the next advance in bridge construction. It has three long stones in line and two primitive supports in the water.

Some of these ancient bridges are, of course, broken; but the famous clapper bridge* over the East Dart, near Postbridge on Dartmoor, is in an excellent state of preservation and is even more impressive than the Weaver's. It, also, has three heavy table slabs of granite, each about fifteen feet long and some six feet wide. The supporting piers,

* These " clapper bridges " were formerly called " Cyclopean "— a term in architecture which has come to be generally used for a wall of large, irregular stones, unhewn and uncemented. The term originated in Greece, where structures of this kind were fabled to have been the work of the Cyclopes, or one-eyed giants.

two of which are in the water, are made of somewhat similar stones piled one on top of the other, each pier having five stones, plac   lengthwise up and down stream. There are several other clappers to be seen on Dartmoor, in a more or less complete state, the one that crosses the Walla Brook having only a single slab, over which man and beast used to pass. If you linger a while in the company of these ancient bridges you can almost picture the shaggy ponies of the fiercely independent miners of the West stepping nimbly across with their burdens of tin.

Pack-horse bridges, many fine specimens of which can still be seen all over the country, are also survivals of the days when most of the country's trade was carried on by horse transport, and several of these picturesque old structures are still in use. They are, naturally, very narrow, barely four feet wide, as they were only built to permit of the passage of the files of horses bearing bales of wool or pedlars' merchandise.

Tradition, so often wrong, would claim an early date for the many " Roman " bridges. There are certainly traces of Roman work here and there ; but many of the so-called Roman bridges are not Roman at all. They mostly date from the seventeenth century and later, and owe their name to the ignorance of antiquarians deceived by the use of the round arch that supplanted the mediæval pointed one.

STOPHAM BRIDGE.

MORE TREASURES

MONNOW BRIDGE, MONMOUTH.

It was not until the advent of the wheeled vehicle that bridge building began in earnest in Britain, but it is difficult to determine who built the first bridge for the passage of vehicular traffic.

Monastic records, however, appear to indicate that the monks, those prolific builders of the Middle Ages, were pioneers in the good work. The Rule of St. Benedict provided that the monks were to entertain and assist travellers, of whatsoever degree, and what more practical way of conferring benefits upon wayfarers than the building of bridges over rivers, that so frequently proved to be obstacles in the traveller's way? Sometimes a chapel was erected on the bridge, so that travellers might show their gratitude by praying for the soul of the founder. Some bridges were built as thank-offerings for escapes or deliverances, others in fulfilment of a vow, while many were erected simply as acts of charity.

Bridges were occasionally of great strategic importance, and so were sometimes fortified, as in the case of the fine mediæval bridge over the River Monnow, Monmouth. Here a splendid fortified gateway, complete with grooves for portcullis and holes for boiling oil and such-like amenities, frowns on the traveller. Unfortunately, this is the only example of a fortified bridge remaining in the United Kingdom to-day. Our coaching forefathers evidently found them a serious obstruction, and it is surprising to find even this one left.

So close is the connection between the general development of civilisation and the development of the bridge that we can best tell the age of a bridge by measuring its girth of masonry. Occasionally, a bridge, or part of a bridge, has a date carved on it ; more often there is some old written record of building or repair work. Yet even when such records exist it is often difficult to say whether the date they give is that at which the foundations were first put down and the arches first built.

The distinguishing feature of most early bridges, i.e. the small narrow arch, is due to the difficulties of the designers of the time, who had not the means or the knowledge to make an arch of wide span, and so were tied to the plan of a succession of small arches and, therefore, a large number of piers. The gradual widening of the average span, and the gradual narrowing of the pier, therefore, give us much surer evidence of the age of bridges than many other features of construction. In the British Isles the arches start from the neighbourhood of 25 feet, in about the year 1200, to reach a maximum of 75 feet about the middle of the eighteenth century, when modern engineering had its birth. Since then the increase has progressed in width with startling rapidity. During the last few years, several splendid new bridges have been built ; but to the wayfarer it is the picturesque old structures, that are so often destroyed to make way for these modern erections, that give the real joy of " crossing the stream." For centuries they have stood, requiring from time to time only those repairs which, in the natural order of things, they need, and we may well do our best to preserve them for the sake of the strange charm and fine beauty of their ancient workmanship.

DEW PONDS

On the chalk downs of Southern England from Sussex to the Marlborough and Wiltshire Hills are certain ponds to which the country folk attribute almost magical powers.

It is claimed, for instance, that although these ponds are invariably found high up on the hills, far from the shade of trees or protecting copse, where no streams have ever flowed, they seldom if ever dry up even when the valleys are parched and the springs reduced to mere trickles.

Tradition, or long usage, has given to them the name of Dew Ponds, and romance has attributed certain of the older ones to the work of Stone Age men.

There is, of course, no record of the making of the first Dew Pond; but in Neolithic times, when most of the country was covered with forest in which lurked wolves and other fierce animals, the early men made their homes on the highest portions of the downs and it may be that these prehistoric folk learned the secret of securing the water they needed for themselves and their cattle on these exposed heights.

A DEW POND.

The secret of the making of these ponds is still known to a few and occasionally a new pond is constructed, or an existing one repaired, by some wandering rural expert.

The general method is to dig a saucer-shaped bed on some part of the downs where mist is apt to collect early on summer mornings. In this hollow, after the chalk and flints have been well rammed, is placed a good layer of straw or reeds on top of which is puddled a covering of clay and in some of the more modern dew ponds a final coating of concrete is used. All are wrought with experience and craft that are a heritage from the past, and then left to dry.

Then, when once the pond has filled (occasionally assisted by artificial means) there will always be water for the cattle to drink, even though no rains fall and the torrid sun pours down its relentless heat day after day.

It would be incorrect to say that there are no dry dew ponds, for they are often to be seen on the hills. But the reason is not far to seek. Once the bed of the pond is cracked or broken the water soon trickles through and the pond naturally fails. That is why a number of dew ponds are fenced, to prevent heavy cattle from wading into them and damaging the bottom.

Scientists have spent many years in trying to probe the mystery of how and whence the water comes that fills these lonely hollows of the hills but so far without success.

The generally accepted explanation is, however, that on a warm summer's day the ground round the pond is warmed ; but its heat cannot get to the clay bed of the pond because of the non-conducting nature of the layer of straw. Therefore when night falls, the cooler clay attracts more moisture from the atmosphere, and so counteracts the evaporation under the hottest of days.

But whatever their origin, or the mystery of the water supply, this much appears to be beyond dispute—that they have stood on the hills thousands of years before men sought to explain them.

THE DOWNS

While we are on the Downs, have you ever thought when struggling up some steep slope in Sussex or standing gazing with rapture at some beautiful view from the top of the North Downs, why these famous chalk hills are called " Downs " when they seem to be all " ups " ?

To find an explanation you must delve right back to the days of the Ancient Britons, when much of the country was forest and swamp, homesteads and encampments were usually built on hills or high ground and were called " downs " by the inhabitants, not " tuns " or " hams " or " burghs " as the Saxons called their dwelling places, until as time went on the hill on which these encampments stood, themselves became known as " Downs " and the name has persisted to our own times.

CHAPTER IV

THE VILLAGE GREEN

To the true wayfarer our beautiful old villages and smaller country towns are not merely places to obtain refreshments, but wonderful store houses holding many valuable relics of our country's past history, in fact a number of them have treasures that are rarely to be found in museums, such as stocks, ducking stools, lock-ups, etc. Such relics, if only they were able to speak, could tell stories that have never found their way into history books.

The village green formerly played a much more important part in the life of the community than is the case to-day. It was often the scene of rough sport and even still rougher justice ; but the ancient and—happily—bygone customs have left relics of great interest, and much pleasure can be had by hunting out their history and significance.

THE STOCKS

One of the oldest forms of punishment was to be placed in the stocks. A number of these old structures are still to be seen in our villages, many of them in an excellent state of preservation, and in several examples, whipping posts are also attached.

Stocks were usually made of stout timber, with a wooden seat for the culprit to sit on ,but one or two

OLD STOCKS AND WHIPPING POST,
AT ALDBURY, HERTS.

examples made of iron are in existence. Referring to the illustration of a wooden example, it will be seen that the contrivance consists of two massive boards with semi-circular holes cut in them. These were fitted together and padlocked so as to hold the legs of the evil doer just above the feet.

It was mostly for minor offences, such as drunkenness or petty theft, that people were placed in the stocks. The chief object of the punishment was to shame the culprit by bringing him into ridicule, and the unhappy wretch would receive scant mercy at the hands of the inhabitants if he were at all unpopular.

That stocks were used by the Anglo-Saxons is proved by their often figuring in drawings of the period (see Harleian MSS. No. 65), although there seems to be no record of the first use of them in England. However, in the second Statute of Labourers (1350), provision is made for applying the stocks to unruly artificers ; it further stated that stocks should be set up in every town between the passing of the Act and the following Pentecost ; but the Act appears to have been ill observed, for in 1376 the Commons again prayed Edward III that stocks should be set up in every village.

The duty of providing and maintaining the stocks generally devolved upon the inhabitants, and some of the old records of orders for their repair or renewal are amusing. For instance, one of the Presentments made by the Leet Jury at Portsmouth in 1629 reads : " Wee give a paine to ye Chamberlaine of this Towne for ye time beinge that he doe make up a sufficient paier of stocks for this Towne for ye punishinge of ofendors (according to ye statute in ye case provided) betweene this and our Ladye Day next in paine to lose xxs."

Punishment by means of the stocks has never been expressly abolished by act of Parliament, but it gradually declined about the beginning of the nineteenth century, though there is a recorded case of its use so late as 1865 at Rugby.

THE PILLORY

The Pillory was another instrument of punishment formerly used in England. It seems to have existed before the Norman Conquest, and pillories are still to be seen in several parts of the country. A pillory consisted generally of a frame of wood, supported by posts and provided with holes similar to the stocks but through which the head and hands of the offender were put, and in which they remained fixed for the time appointed in the sentence. In this manner the prisoner was exposed to public view and was frequently subjected to grievous insults or even outrage at the hands of the populace.

The Pillory was originally intended, according to the Statute of the Pillory, for forestallers, that is, tradesmen who cornered the market and put up the price of goods, for users

THE DUCKING STOOL AT LEOMINSTER.

of deceitful weights, perjurers, forgers and all such dishonourable offenders and was confined to these classes until 1637. From that date, restriction was put upon the Press, and all who printed books without a licence were put in the pillory. At that time it became the favourite mode of punishing libellers (or those who were considered to be such by the government), authors and publishers of seditious pamphlets, and of critics of the government. Many eminent men were accordingly, from this time, pilloried, among whom may be mentioned Leighton, the father of the Archbishop ; Lilburn and Varton, the printers ; Prynne ; and Daniel Defoe, the author of Robinson Crusoe.

Frequently when the sufferers were popular favourites, or had at least numerous supporters, they were shaded from the sun, fed, and otherwi e carefully attended to ; while the applause and sympathy of the crowd converted the intended punishment into a triumph. Such men as Titus Oates, however, who were objects of popular hatred and disgust, were pelted with rotten eggs, garbage and stones, and it is on record that several culprits were killed in the pillory by the brutality of the mob.

As an instrument for the public punishment of criminals,

the pillory was finally abolished in Britain in the first year of Queen Victoria's reign, 1837.

A few pillories still survive in this country. One fine specimen in good preservation is to be seen at Coleshill, in Warwickshire, and another at Rye, in Sussex, is said to have been used as late as 1813.

THE DUCKING STOOL

The ducking stool was yet another cruel apparatus used in this country in bygone days for the punishment of dishonest tradesmen, quarrelsome married folk and women who were scolds. In later years it was almost exclusively used for women. These quaint structures take various forms. In the earlier examples they consisted of a rough, strong chair attached to one end of a beam, which worked on a pivot on a post embedded in the ground at the edge of the bank of a pond or stream. The offender was placed in the chair and securely tied with cords. Those who were to carry out the punishment then took hold of a chain or rope at the opposite end which lowered the arm and gave the prisoner a ducking on the see-saw principle.

In later examples wheels were sometimes fitted to the beam so that the offender could first be dragged through the streets in the chair before receiving the ducking in the pond, for which job there was no lack of willing helpers.

THE OLD BULL RING AT HORSHAM, SUSSEX.

Another form of ducking stool consisted of an upright and a transverse beam, either movable or fixed, from which the chair was suspended by a rope or chain.

The practice of ducking is believed to have commenced in the latter part of the fifteenth century and prevailed

THE QUINTAIN, OFFHAM, KENT.

generally until the early part of the eighteenth century, although a few isolated cases have been recorded as late as the beginning of the nineteenth, the last cases being those of a Mrs. Gamble, at Plymouth in 1808; Jennie Pipes " a notorious scold," 1809, and Sarah Lecke, 1817, both at Leominster. In the last case the water in the port was so low that the victim could not be ducked and she was merely wheeled round the town in the chair.

BULL-BAITING

On several of our village greens can be seen the old bull ring, preserved as a memorial of the " good old days " when bull-baiting was a popular sport. There is one at Horsham, Sussex, where, in 1813, the last bull was baited, and another at Brading in the Isle of Wight.

Bull-baiting was a national pastime in England for over six hundred years, and it is almost incredible that such a barbarous sport should have been held to be legal until 1835.

As a rule the ring was fastened into a stout post driven into the ground on the village green and the bull secured by a length of chain about 20 feet long, fastened to a stout leather collar round its neck. The chain was usually connected to the ring by a swivel, which enabled the bull to move freely round to face his antagonists. The bulldog's part in the sport was to try and seize the animal by its nose and then to hold on, termed " pinning and holding."

The dog got at close quarters with the bull by creeping on its belly close to the ground (this was termed playing low), and making its final spring when the bull's nose was exposed. The bull tried to protect its nose, often making a hole in the soft ground with its feet to rest his nose in, and watched for the least mistake on the bulldog's part, with head lowered to toss or gore it the instant the opportunity arose. When the bulldog made a " pin " and " held," the bull tried frantically to free itself, but the pain being so excruciating, it was rendered helpless almost at once. On the other hand, if the dog did not make a " hold," or missed altogether, the bull had him before he could recover, and often tossed a dog high in the air. The bulldog had a handler, who wisely kept just out of reach of the bull. If the dog was tossed, the handler made a last effort to save its life by catching it on his shoulder, and thus breaking its fall.

As opposed to such cruel sports as bull-baiting, it is pleasant to remember the Maying, when young men and women went into the woods and returned with branches of leaves and flowers and a birch tree for the maypole. More permanent poles were erected in later years, and I believe the tallest now remaining is that at Shillingstone, Dorset.

THE QUINTAIN

A unique sporting relic to be found on the village green at Offham, near Maidstone, Kent, is a quintain post, the only one of its kind surviving in England. In the Middle Ages tilting at the quintain was a common knightly exercise, in preparation for jousting at the tournaments. Later, during the seventeenth and eighteenth centuries, this sport became a favourite at country weddings.

The quintain varied a good deal in form in different periods and in different places. At first it was merely an

THE LOCK-UP AT CASTLE CARY.

THE WAYFARER'S BOOK

upright post with a shield on top but later it took the form of an upright post surmounted by " a crossbar " turning on a pivot, which had at one end a flat board, at the other a bag of sand. The object of the rider was to gallop beneath it at full tilt, striking the board with his lance at such speed that he was past before the hanging sandbag on the other end whirled round and struck him on the back or head.

It was an excellent device for discomfiting the unskilled man-at-arms and must have been a great thrill for the onlookers. Sometimes a cap or other small article attached to the cross bar was removed on the point of the lance, while at full gallop, without causing the arm of the quintain to revolve.

THE LOCK-UP

It was before the days of organised police that local authorities took it upon themselves to provide a " pound " for the poor animal who chanced to stray from the pastures of its owner and a " lock-up " for the poor wretch who chanced to stray from the paths of righteousness. The lock-up was only used as a temporary place of detention, until such time as the malefactor could be removed to the county gaol. Frequently this departure from the rightful course was caused by " supping " too deeply, and the unsteady fellow was run into the " cage " in order to cool his heels—and head—before the local magistrate had a look at him in the morning. Petty offenders were generally released after a day or so.

Quite a number of these diminutive prisons are still in existence and can often be found close to the village green. In shape they are a mixture of bee-hive, pepper-pot and Eskimo dwelling. The old lock-up on the village green at Shenley, Hertfordshire, is a typical example. It is circular in plan and has an arched doorway with a heavy oak door. There are two small windows cut through the wall, which is eighteen inches thick, one on either side of the door. Over the right-hand window is written the exhortation, " Be sober. Be Vigilant," and over the left-hand window is another, " Do Well and Fear not," with the date, 1810. It has, in common with most other " lock-ups," an ornament on the top very like a pawn in the game of chess.

Shrewton (Wilts), Alton (Staffs.) and Castle Cary (Somerset), also possess excellent lock-ups, built on the circular plan. The last named was erected in 1779 and cost £23 to build. The walls are three feet thick and lighting and ventilation are provided by a small grating over the door. The design of a modern policeman's helmet may well have been taken from the roof of this tiny prison.

These buildings would, as a matter of course, be plain and solid; but there is one at Lingfield, Surrey, of unique construction. Sandwiched between an ancient oak and the village pond, this small, church-like building was used as a lock-up during the last century. It is generally thought to have come into existence as a wayside shrine, and only to have been adapted as a village "cage" when necessity arose. The design certainly seems to confirm this view; and in addition the words "St. Peter's Cross" are carved upon one of the stones in the wall.

THE VILLAGE CAGE. LINGFIELD, SURREY.

THE POUND

Thus, upon the village common
        By the school-boys he was found;
And the wise men, in their wisdom,
        Put him straightway into pound.
                LONGFELLOW, "Pegasus in Pound."

The "pound" usually a piece of enclosed land, set apart by law, in which stray or trespassing cattle were detained or impounded.

Whenever a stranger's or neighbour's cattle trespassed on another's land, the latter could seize them, take them to the pound, and keep them there till the damage done by them had been paid for by the owner.

At one time there was a distinction between pound overt, or common pound, and pound covert, or closed pound ; in the former case, the owner of the impounded cattle was allowed to feed and water his beasts while they were in the pound, in fact it was his duty to do so ; but he was not allowed that privilege in the latter case. Now, however, it is compulsory for the impounder, in both cases to supply the cattle with food, otherwise he incurs a penalty, if the impounded cattle are not sufficiently fed. A stranger who feeds them may not only trespass on lands to do so, but can recover the costs from the owner of the beasts. This was formerly an important head of law, and it is not obsolete, for the power to impound stray cattle still exists, though common pounds are disappearing, for, in point of law, they are no longer necessary, as the impounder is now allowed to put the cattle in his own stable or field.

VILLAGE PUMPS AND WELLS

In days gone by the village pump has been an object of ridicule. Why, I do not know, because a pump is a most useful object. It makes the drawing of water easy in those pleasant, but benighted, places which have no up-to-date water supply (and no corresponding up-to-date water rate !)

Although modern water engineering is rapidly superseding the village pump, the wayfarer can still find some picturesque pumps and wells of such antiquity that some of them were in use when the Romans landed in Britain, while early mediæval examples are common. A number of these are still in everyday use at the present time, and the water which they supply frequently possesses excellent properties.

The ancient wells and springs of London would provide material for an article by themselves. Many of them are perpetuated in the names of streets, buildings or districts. The Holy Well in Holywell Street (demolished to widen the Strand), for instance, reminds us of a well revived by the Canterbury Pilgrims. Clerke's Well, and the village of Clerkenwell to which it gave its name, have alike disappeared ; although Clerkenwell Road is still an important thoroughfare.

St. Clement's Well, near the Strand, was described by a

ST. KEYNE'S WELL, NEAR LOOE IN CORNWALL.

writer in the year 1180 as " Sweet, cleare and wholesome."
It is no longer traceable and has probably been built over,
a fate which many other London wells have suffered. Thus
Sadler's Well is now in the basement of a house in Lloyd's
Row, almost opposite Sadler's Wells Theatre, and the famous
Chalybeate Well at Hampstead is likewise hidden in a house
in Well Walk.

Aldgate Pump still stands, but it is now a topographical
symbol rather than a well. It is, however, still an interesting
relic of the civic enterprise of past ages.

Many ancient wells are still regarded by some of the older
country folk as sacred or holy wells. They attribute to
these wells many quaint and mysterious qualities and regard
the waters as possessing miraculous healing properties.

A law was issued in 1018 forbidding the worship of trees,
stones and wells ; but it was in vain. For centuries afterwards sufferers visited the Holy Pool of Stoathfellow, in
Perthshire, to be healed of various illnesses ; while even
to-day the well of Dwynwen, she whom the Welsh bards
called the " Saint of Love," has its occasional votaries.

The cult of water worship began when the Egyptians
realised their debt to the Nile, and even now has no small
place in the folklore of the world. It was strong in Britain
in mediæval days, when England was very poorly supplied
with good drinking water. Often there was only one well
in the whole of a large village or market town. It is not
difficult to realise, therefore, how, originally, such an
important water supply would be placed under the protection
of some favourite saint or holy person associated with the
district, to guard the well from all evil and polluting influences.
As time went on, the patron saint of the well would be
imbued in the mind of the more religiously-minded folk
with the power of effecting cures of certain diseases through
the medium of the water from the well. Thus we see how
there came into being the many picturesque " holy wells "
which add their old-world charm, and the strangely fragrant
aroma of their antiquity, to many of our rural areas.

Many of these old wells are surrounded by quaint stories
and legends. The Holy Well of St. Keyne's is perhaps one
of the most celebrated. It is situated about half a mile from
the village of that name near Looe in Cornwall. St. Keyne
was one of St. Brechou's twenty-six children, an exceptionally
lovely and pure maid who performed miracles.

CHAPTER V

ALONG THE ROAD

" The rule of the road is a paradox quite,
  Both in riding and driving along;
If you keep to the left, you are sure to be right,
  If you keep to the right, you are wrong."

EARLY EIGHTEENTH CENTURY RHYME.

MILESTONES

In all that has been done of late years in the way of country-side preservation and the care of ancient monuments, no general effort seems to have been made on behalf of some of our oldest friends, the milestones. It is sad to see, in many parts of the country, what a state of decay many of them are in, and it is to be feared that most of these stones may in time disappear altogether. The Romans well understood the value of milestones, and all their roads on the Continent were flanked with pillars erected at equal distances which marked the number of miles from Rome. It was natural, then, that when they came to Britain and built their military roads some 2000 years ago, they set up milestones to measure the distances along these roads. What happened to these milestones we do not know, but presumably the system fell into disuse after their departure and the stones perished as did so many of the other Roman works in Britain.

In the Museum at Lincoln can be seen one of the few authentic Roman milestones (*Miliarium*). It was found near the cross-roads at Bailgate; and gives the distance of Lincoln from Littleborough-on-Trent as fourteen miles. In the Norman Church at Wroxeter is another Roman milestone.

There is considerable doubt as to the origin of the famous London Stone which occupies a position in the wall of St. Swithin's Church in Cannon Street, but it is considered by some authorities to date from Roman times, and to have formed the central milestone from which all distances were measured. It is a fact that the Romans placed a stone in such a position in all the countries they conquered.

The Roman mile was 1,000 paces, and 725 Roman miles were equivalent to 665 of our English miles.

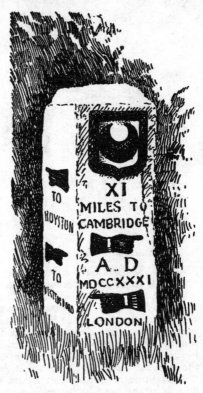

Each British milestone is said by some to be a monument to our obstinate disregard of the metric system, and I am afraid that the accuracy of many old milestones is very much to be doubted. One choice example, for instance, is to be seen outside the Red Lion Hotel at Atherstone, Warwickshire, which calmly states that London, Lincoln and Liverpool are each 100 miles away. Lincoln is less than 70 miles away, London is 102 miles, and Liverpool is a few miles over the 100.

In days gone by there was a decree that the king could not travel more than fifty miles away from London without a minister. In the Georgian era this restriction was such

MILESTONE ON CAMBRIDGE TO LONDON ROAD.

an annoyance to royalty, that although Brighton was fifty-one and three quarter miles from London, all the milestones stated it was less than fifty!

FINGERPOST AND SIGNPOST.

But before we smile at the above variations we should remember that although the English ordinary mile contains 1,760 yards, the English geographical mile has 2,096, the Admiralty mile 2,027, and the nautical 2,026.

Some of the oldest milestones in England (excluding those set up by the Romans) are to be found along the high road going from Cambridge to the village of Barkway, a distance of about sixteen miles. There were sixteen stones originally, but some of them have now disappeared. One, however, which is to be found about three miles from Royston, is in quite good condition. The crest upon it is that of Trinity Hall, and the reason of the decoration is that one of the dons of the Hall left a sum of money for the repair of the road—over which he had often travelled—and for the erection of sixteen " respectable " mileston ; and in 1731 the more decorative examples were put up in place of the previous insignificant types. It was not, however, until the seventeenth century that it was thought necessary to take much trouble over the milestones on our roads. Then the passing of the General Turnpike Act in 1766 made their provision compulsory.

To the Wayfarer our ancient milestones are always interesting, and not infrequently beautiful, and like Dick Whittington of old a man may rest upon a milestone before he passes on his journey. They are the present, with the past on one side of them and the future on the other. " Thus far," they say, " have you come ; thus far remains for you to go." For them there is always a beginning and an end.

FINGERPOSTS AND SIGNPOSTS

Fingerposts are often erroneously described as signposts. Correctly speaking, a signpost is a post on which a sign hangs, such as is to be seen outside many old village inns. A fingerpost proper is a post set up, generally where roads cross or divide, to show the direction to certain places.

Some of the older fingerposts in the remote parts of the country have rings with which to tether horses, for it must be remembered that fingerposts were primarily intended for the guidance of horse-back travellers. It was for this reason also that the height of a fingerpost arm was always fixed at eye-level to a mounted man. In some parts of the country, where the district is liable to flooding, the fingerposts were marked with flood levels, but the improvement in land drainage in modern times accounts for the discontinuance of these marks.

In reference to fingerposts, an amusing story is told in Yorkshire of a wayfarer who, on asking the way to a village, was informed that he would find a " parson " at the top of the hill which would tell him the way to go. " Your clergy seem very obliging," replied the inquirer. He was then

A TYPICAL UPPING BLOCK.

63

told that in that district fingerposts were called " parsons " because they always point the way but do not follow it themselves.

UPPING BLOCKS

An interesting reminder of more leisurely days, when much of the travelling was done by coach or on horseback, are the up ing or mounting blocks which one comes across by the roadside in many parts of the country.

These old blocks consisted of two or more flat stones of different lengths laid one upon the other so as to form a solid flight of steps. They were placed in a convenient position so as to enable travellers to mount their steeds with comparative ease. London has a number of them still in existence. Several are scattered around Hyde Park, two are in St. James's Square and one in Waterloo Place, erected in 1830 by desire of the Duke of Wellington to assist clubmen of his day to mount.

One of the oldest of these upping blocks can be seen on a wide stretch of grass by the side of the road leading from Banbury to Daventry—near Aston-le-Walls. This mounting block bears the inscription :

> " Thomas Knight (or Hight) of Warden
> Set up this, July the 30th, 1659."

By " Warden " is meant the neighbouring village of Chipping Warden.

Another specimen standing beside the Great North Road at Wansfield, near Stamford, is a stone marking the eig y-first mile from London, which bears the date 1708 and the initials E.B. It served in Georgian days both as a milestone and a mounting block, having been one of many such set up at frequent intervals along the Road ; but this is the sole survivor. The initials stand for Edmund Boulter, by whose forethought travellers in those far from easy times were able to pursue their difficult journey with more certainty.

Another specimen in a very good state of preservation is to be seen close to the famous triangular bridge which stands high and dry in the village of Crowland.

An exceedingly quaint upping block stands outside a wayside inn at a place called Jackament's Bottom, on the main road between Cirencester and Tetbury, placed there in 1766 by some thoughtful person whose name has long since been forgotten. It is quite different from most other blocks, being three and a half feet high and obviously constructed for the use of coach passengers, rather than for horsemen.

CITY POSTS

At a country house dinner party in Kent I well remember, the conversation had for some time centred round various points concerning the Highway Code, when it gradually drifted, as conversation often does on such occasions, to cars, horses, road improvements and kindred subjects.

Then, the lady sitting on my right

A City Post.

remarked that she had seen a quaint old iron post during one of her journeys, which she was told had something to do with road improvements, but she was unable to discover in exactly what way. Had I ever come across one?

Having made a hobby of collecting information and photographs of similar quaint objects I was able to inform

STONE STILE AT FROYLE, HAMPSHIRE.

her that the post she had discovered was known as a City Post. These posts, bearing the City of London arms and " Act 24 & 25 Vict. Cap 42 " can be found in many odd places within the Metropolitan Police district of 1861. Two can be seen at Downe in Kent, another at Chertsey Weir and quite a number on Oxshott and Walton Heaths. They were placed there in 1861, under an Act of that year which gave power to the Corporation to renew duties on wine and coal for the purpose of road improvements, etc.

The wine duty started under an Act of William and Mary, the coal duty went back in ancient rights of meterage of all coal coming into the port of London, such rights being definitely recognised by a charter of James I. After the Fire of London a duty was levied on the vend and delivery of coal to raise money for rebuilding the city and later was applied to the acquisition of open spaces.

STILES

STILE, STIL, *n.* A Saxon stiegel, a step, a ladder, from *stigan*, to mount or climb, which appears also in stair, stirrup. A step or series of steps, or a frame of bars and steps, for ascending and descending in getting over a fence.

Thus says the Dictionary.

But to the wayfarer a stile is often a thing of beauty and romance as well as a convenient place to rest. Next to the footpath, whose inseparable companion it is, the stile is the wayfarer's most ancient heritage, and like the footpath varies considerably in form and substance, the nature of the land being often reflected in the material used.

Broadly speaking, there are three kinds of stiles, namely, step-stiles, V-stiles, and ladder stiles.

The wooden form, with its one or two cross steps, to be seen in the southern agricultural and wooded countries, is probably the most familiar, and is a friendly affair, a place for loitering. Strong for the purpose, it yet has a certain charm that is lacking in its northern brethren. In its sturdiness it claims kinship with the famous " wooden walls " of England, and is as much a part of the countryside as the sailing-ship was of the sea.

Another wooden stile occasionally seen in Sussex, Kent and Herefordshire, is known as a " Squeezer." This is a V-shaped stile allowing the rambler to go through but effectively barring the way to cattle or wheeled traffic.

This type has its stone counterpart in some districts of Derbyshire where it is usually referred to as " The fat man's misery," a very apt description, for the "extensive" traveller is certainly faced with a problem when confronted with one. The stone wall country, however, provides a pleasant variation, in the form of small wooden ladders by which the walls can be surmounted. They range from rustic ones of tree branches, with their projecting ends lashed together like the fingers of the path-ends clasped in greeting across the

A " SQUEEZER " STILE.

dividing stones, to elaborate affairs of smooth planks complete with handrails.

The stiles of the north and west are usually of much sterner stuff than the southern types.

In Cornwall, Wales and the Pennines, slate and stone predominate. All who are familiar with Cornwall will know the stone ladders that are set in the high hedges, and the curious stiles that consist of slabs of granite laid flat like sleepers. In Devon the walls have stones sticking out at right angles, often awkward obstacles to negotiate, especially in wet weather.

A quaint carved stone stile of a kind unfortunately rather rare, can be seen near Froyle, in Hampshire, while the unique clapper stile at Linton, Cambridgeshire, is believed to be only one of three in the whole country. The strange habit of this type of stile is that it collapses directly any weight is put upon the top bar.

How many purely local types of stiles there are to be seen in the country districts of England would be almost impossible to say. One such local form I came across during my wanderings in Berkshire. It seemed to be a combination of two other types of pathway barriers.

The post-and-rail arrangement, consisting of two upright posts, with a gap between narrow enough to prevent vehicles passing through yet wide enough to admit pedestrians and difficult enough to baffle straying animals, is found in many places.

The upright stone slab placed across a gap where the footpath passes through a wall is often to be seen on the Cotswolds, where it is known as a sheep-stile, because it is designed to prevent sheep from wandering through the gap where the footpath runs. A person can step over the slab, although in many cases it is a good high step, but a sheep will not jump it. In Berkshire, however, the people have made doubly sure of restricting footpaths to their proper use by setting across them both the post-and-rail arrangement and the upraised stone slab.

THE LYCH-GATE AND OTHERS

Every wayfarer knows what a lych-gate is ; but there are probably some who do not know the meaning of the name, or anything else about these picturesque features of our old

A LYCH-GATE.

villages, beyond the fact that they are usually decorative roofed entrance-gates to churchyards.

The oldest and most beautiful of these structures were not built, however, purely for decoration, as many might imagine, but for a very definite purpose.

In former days it was at the lych-gate that the coffin was rested awhile before being taken into the church for the first part of the funeral service. In some of the older lych-gates the original lych-stone or coffin rest is still retained, but there are not many left now, as most of them were taken away in the eighteenth century. It was thought, quite naturally perhaps, that they hindered worshippers making their way into the church.

The beautiful old lych-gate at Chiddingford is one example where the lych-stone is still preserved, and there is another at Bolney, in Sussex. The gate around this old stone is of unusually massive proportions.

The commonest type of lych-gate in England was built in the form of a timbered porch and very often enhanced with carvings of notable merit. Many lych-gates of this type date back four or five hundred years. A different type is that which combines with other buildings and so forms a covered passage-way to the churchyard. Most of these date from early mediæval times and possess a rare and

A GATE USED FOR COUNTING SHEEP.

distinctive beauty. The gate at Penshurst, in the heart of Kent, is one of this type and is surrounded by beautiful houses of the early Tudor period.

In days gone by a curious superstition attached itself to these gates. It was that the spirit of the last person buried in the churchyard hovered round the lych-gate ready to escort his successor to the grave.

The word " lych " is derived from the German " leiche," which means a corpse. Sometimes the English derivation is spelt with an " i " instead of a " y." Many other words prefixed by " lych " are invariably associated with death.

The lych-gate is by no means the only gate with some peculiar interest that can be discovered during a ramble. You may occasionally see one having only two horizontal bars with a considerable space underneath. This gate is used by a farmer when he wishes to separate certain sheep from a flock. Getting his dog to round them up and drive them to the gate, he selects the animals required as they come forward, and by pressing their heads down slightly pushes them under the gate. An ordinary gate which has to be opened is of little use as it would be almost impossible to prevent the animals from rushing through after each other ; but a gate of the type mentioned will keep the sheep in, for they will rarely pass under without having their heads pressed down and being pushed.

Another variety of gate that almost every wayfarer will meet is the type technically known as a cage-wicket, that is a foot-gate which swings within an angular or circular cage. It is designed to prevent cattle passing from one field to another, while giving easy access to human beings. This type of gate is called a kissing-gate by the country folk, for as only one person at a time can pass through, the bold swain was wont to demand toll of the bashful maiden on the other side of the gate.

There are, of course, dozens of gates which might be classed more as oddities than any particular type. Many of these are connected with trades and were designed to catch the eye of possible customers.

One curious survival of early days which is often seen on gateways is the large stone ball set on the top of a gatepost. The usage of this method of finish is really a relic of barbarian days, when victors in battle decorated their doorways with the heads of the vanquished.

Chapter VI

ODDMENTS ABOUT THE COUNTRYSIDE

THE WEATHERCOCK

" O weathercock on the village spire,
With your golden feathers all on fire
Tell me, what can you see from your perch
Above there over the tower of the Church?"

LONGFELLOW.

Now that we have only to turn on the wireless or glance at a newspaper in order to learn in which direction the wind is blowing and the direction it is likely to take for the next few hours, the old Weathervane is apt to be forgotten.

Weathervanes were in use as far back as Saxon days, and were extensively employed during the prevalence of the Perpendicular and Elizabethan styles of architecture. On towers, castles, and secular buildings the usual form was that of a banner; while on churches it was generally a representation of a male of the barn-door fowl, and was thus often spoken of as a weathercock.

THE WEATHERCOCK.

There is a popular idea which associates the cock on the church steeple with Peter's denial of Jesus :

> " Jesus said unto him, Verily I say unto thee, that this night, before the cock crow, thou shalt deny me thrice."
>
> (MATTHEW XXVI, 34.)

and that it was chosen as the design of the weathervane as a reminder and warning to the people not to do the same. But this idea is probably an afterthought, for the cock on the weathervane has earlier religious associations.

The cock was sacred in the religion of Zoroaster, and in one of the ancient sacred books of the Parsees, who worshipped the forbears of our domestic fowls, the following lines appear :

> " Who is he who sets the world in motion, a mighty speared and lordly god ? It is Parodaro, the cock that lifts up his voice against the mighty dawn."

In very ancient times a representation of a cock was placed on the tops of sacred trees and was supposed to drive away evil spirits and ward off calamities. Probably it was placed on churches for the same reason.

STADDLES

In many parts of the country, especially in the Cotswold districts, in Sussex and parts of Yorkshire, may be seen large stones some two or three feet in height, similar in shape to giant toadstools. These peculiar stones are called " staddles," from the Anglo-Saxon word " stathol," meaning foundation, something that supports ; and they are used as foundation stones on which hay and wheat stacks are supported. Small barns are also built on them.

Staddle barns were originally intended as granaries, and the stones serve the purpose of making them rat-proof, for rats, however cunning they may be, cannot climb upside down, and are therefore unable to get round the large cap of the " toadstool."

Staddles serve the same purpose when used as supports for hay or wheat stacks, and also keep the stack well away from the wet ground in a rainy season. In building a stack, beams

AN OLD STADDLE BARN.

are first laid across the tops of the staddles, the hay or wheat then being stacked up on them.

These stone staddles are now becoming favourite garden ornaments, and are often to be seen in the corners of lawns or as decorations at garden gates and steps, and they make very attractive additions to either a modern garden or one of the old cottage-garden style. They are, I understand, actually being manufactured especially for that purpose.

SCARECROWS OR BOGLES

The trials of a farmer are never ending; no sooner are the worries of winter over and work on the spring sowings started, than a fresh host of troubles arrive.

Rooks, starlings, wood pigeons and many other feathered thieves now become the great problem, for the birds seem to organise their marauding parties and to increase in guile and wisdom as the days pass. All manner of quaint contraptions are employed to scare them from the growing crops, with varying success, and a country walk will usually reveal quite a number of these strange devices to an observant rambler.

There is, of course, the old familiar scarecrow, or " bogle " as the Scotsman calls it, with ragged, flapping garments and battered top hat, which is usually set up in the centre of a field where the crops are. These grotesque figures often show ingenuity, even artistry, in their design, but whether they are really of much use in scaring the birds is doubtful. From my observations the birds seem, for the most part, to treat this colossal fraud as a huge joke, for on one of my rambles I watched, with much amusement, a bald-faced old rook, far from being terrified by such a " hollow being " perch confidently on a most realistic old scarecrow's shoulder and, after wiping his beak on its outstretched arm, make a vicious dig at the battered old hat and send it flying to the ground.

Noise and movement seem to be the only things which really disturb the avion thieves and a number of bogles are designed with this end in view.

One such device, often seen where peas and such like crops are being grown in cottage gardens, is a complicated arrangement of pieces of glass and tin suspended from a string slung between two stakes and intended either to flash vividly in the sunlight or to jingle in the breeze.

The success of this arrangement depends principally upon its novelty, and a week or so is perhaps the utmost limit of its effective use.

Where smaller birds are concerned, certain colours are often made use of ; sparrows, for instance, seem susceptible to such influence, and a few sheets of bright blue paper hung among the gooseberry or red currant bushes will generally scare them off, while fruit growers use long waving streamers of yellow wood shavings to keep finches away from their cherry trees.

Another device often to be seen in small allotments and gardens is what the country folk call a " tatie bogle." It consists of a potato with feathers stuck into it and suspended on a string from a small stake ; several of these are often stuck about a garden. But the most interesting scarecrow of all is the human variety, with his clappers and quaint rhymes. One does not often meet him these days, but a few years back the sound of his clappers might be heard as he moved among the cherry orchards in Kent during the fruit season or up and down the field after the spring sowing.

The small boys who were engaged for this work were known as "clapper boys," and the clappers they used were made of ash wood, in three pieces, the two tongues half the length of the handle and all loosely jointed by

SCARECROW AND CLAPPER.

pieces of leather. As they went about their task these boys often sung quaint rhymes.

One that I can remember hearing when I was a small boy, ran something like this :

" Hey, you black witches on hedges and ditches,
 I'll rattle my clapper and knock you down back'ards,
 Here's farmer wi' gun, you'll fly and I'll run ! "

Another that I heard from an old man in Berks, who had been employed when a boy of eleven as a scarer at three shillings per week, ran as follows :

" Now all you little blackie tops,
 Pray don't you eat my father's crops,
 While I lie down and take a nap.
   Shoo . . . ha . . . ho,
   Shoo . . . ha . . . ho.

"And if by chance my father should come,
With his cock'd hat and great long gun,
You must fly and I must run,
        Shoo . . . ha . . . ho,
        Shoo . . . ha . . . ho."

HAMMER PONDS

In very early days, much of England was covered with an almost impenetrable mass of trees. Even in Saxon times very little clearing had taken place and the dwellers in the dense forest were often totally unknown to the outer world. We are even told that the old Saxon church at Worth was not included in Domesday Book because William I's commissioners were unaware of its existence.

By mediæval times the ever-increasing use of wood, especially oak, in house building and the construction of ships made considerable inroads into the timbers of the forest ; but it was not until the coming of the Sussex iron industry during the Elizabethan period that the real destruction of the forests started.

The Weald became at that time the "Black Country," and the centre of the iron smelting industry, which extended also into West Kent and certain parts of Surrey. Furnaces sprang up in profusion and the indiscriminate use of timber for fuel, without due consideration for afforestation, combined with the ever increasing need of the Queen's Navy for new ships, had such a devastating effect on the forest that drastic restrictive measures were brought into force. But they were too late ; the forest was irretrievably ruined, and of all the great mass of timber which once covered the Weald we have only such fragments left as St. Leonard's Forest, Ashdown Forest, and the forests of Tilgate, Balcombe and Worth. With the sudden restrictions on their fuel iron-masters were compelled to move their trade northwards where a more plentiful supply of fuel (coal) was obtainable.

Among the relics which this old industry has left us, other than numerous beautiful specimens of iron work, such as quaint fire-backs, tomb plates and elaborate old cannon,* are the Hammer Ponds.

The power necessary for the hammers and draught furnaces was obtained from a mill driven by a head of water

* It is interesting to note that the railings outside St. Paul's Cathedral were cast at Lamberhurst in Kent.

concentrated in one or more of these ponds. John Ray, in his Collection of English Words not generally used, published in 1672, and printed in the Sussex Archæological Collections, mentions the hammer ponds in his account of the methods of the old iron smelters.

" A stream, or a pond with a stream running through it would be dammed, and the fall of water at the lower end would then work two pairs of bellows for the blast for the furnaces and a wheel which raised and let fall a hammer."

Another relic the industry has left scattered over the weald is a wealth of place-names which stir the imagination and give testimony of its former importance. Places now peacefully secluded, which once rang with the noise of the picks and hammers of an iron mine, bear such titles as Furnace Woods, Forge Farm, and Hammerwoods.

As we linger on the wooded slopes surrounding some

THE BOWDER STONE IN BORROWDALE,
IN THE LAKE DISTRICT.

beautiful pond, hidden well away from the beaten track in peace and quietness, it is indeed hard to visualise the district as the centre of a once noisy and thriving industry.

PERCHED BLOCKS

Perched blocks and Rocking Stones, known by the general name of Erratics, are boulders of rock, often of enormous size, found balanced precariously on hillslopes and mountains.

These blocks, as a rule, differ in their mineralogical composition from the rocks in their immediate neighbourhood, for in most cases they have travelled a considerable distance from their original home. In a few instances it is even possible to trace them back to the parent rock.

In a number of cases there are attractive myths and legends, concerning these great boulders, that claim to tell how some of them were transported from distant places and left in their present positions by the careless hand of some long-dead giant. The truth is they are relics of the Great Ice Age, when most of England was covered by an enormous ice sheet. At that time the slowly-moving glaciers, that shaped our hills and carved so many of our beautiful valleys, carried with them during their passage downhill great masses of boulder clay and other debris, until, in the course of time, the ice melted and the enormous boulders and numerous other stones and sand were deposited in parts of the country far from their original home.

Additional proof of glaciation will be revealed by an examination of the surface of some of these boulders ; long scratches will be seen, most of them running parallel to each other and with a deep indentation at one end.

These scratches are indications of the glacier's work, having been caused by the moving masses of ice as it passed over the boulder's surface, dragging pebbles and other rock fragments with it on its passage.

Not infrequently, perched blocks rest only on a very small base and are so delicately balanced that a push is sufficient to set them rocking. Such boulders are usually known as Rocking Stones.

The Lake District has one of the most famous of these great perched blocks in the country. It is known as the Bowder Stone and is in the heart of Borrowdale among the Cumberland mountains. This huge block of stone is computed to weigh some 1,900 tons and is claimed to be the largest piece of detached rock in the land. It measures sixty feet in length by thirty feet in height and rests on a narrow edge less than a yard in width and through a hole near the bottom two persons may clasp hands from either side.

One of the best known Rocking Stones is probably the Logan Rock, to be found not far from Land's End. Perched high above the blue waters of the Channel, this delicately poised rock is estimated to weigh at least seventy tons, yet it can be rocked backwards and forwards in a most curious manner with a comparatively slight push.

Rocking stones are not very rare in this world; but few of them have created such a pother as this one, made early in the last century. Camden started the trouble long ago, when he wrote of it that " though it be of a vast bigness you may yet move it with one finger; notwithstanding which, a great number of men would not be able to remove it." This was repeated and repeated. It grew and grew, until at last Dr. Borlase, the famous writer on Cornwall, wrote: "It is morally impossible that any lever or indeed force, however applied in a mechanical way can remove it from its present position."

This statement very nearly brought about the ruin of the Logan Rock altogether. For in 1824 a young British naval officer, Lieutenant Goldsmith, nephew of the famous Oliver Goldsmith, with the help of ten or twelve naval ratings, caused it to slide into a narrow chasm some distance below.

But such a storm of protest was made to the Naval authorities that the Lieutenant was ordered to replace the stone in its former position at his own expense.

A BENCH MARK.

BENCH MARKS

Bench marks are to be found in all sorts of places—cut on milestones, on the corners of buildings, on posts, under bridges and even cut into living rock.

A bench mark is placed in position by Government surveyors and consists of a broad arrow with a cross-piece along the top, while below are usually the letters B.M. and various numbers. This mark is the Ordnance Datum and is put there to show the height of that particular spot above the Ordnance Datum Bench Mark (or official sea-level).

The Ordnance Datum of Great Britain is taken as the mean level of the sea at Liverpool. The cross-piece along the top is the " bench " or ledge from which the exact height above sea-level has been measured. The broad arrow below it is simply the Government's official mark, the use of which dates from the reign of William III, in the seventeenth century.

A CRUCK-HOUSE.

ODDMENTS ABOUT THE COUNTRYSIDE

CRUCK-HOUSES

The cruck-house is probably the oldest type of dwelling house still surviving in England. The same principle was used in the construction of barns and other farm buildings, and was continued in fairly constant use up to some four hundred years ago ; but it is doubtful whether any true cruck-house in this country has been built since then.

The surviving specimens are mostly to be found in out-of-the-way villages in the southern and central parts of England that have fortunately escaped the mixed blessing of modern development and improvement. In Gloucestershire there are several excellent specimens. Another quite unspoilt example I discovered a few years ago at Winwick, near Warrington ; but in a .number of counties not one single specimen survives. They are, in fact, sufficiently rare to make it worth while for the wayfarer to hunt them out and, if he be photographically minded, to make a " collection " of them, for they are gradually becoming fewer.

The construction of a cruck-house was a very simple affair and probably represents a direct development from very primitive forms of habitation such as shelters made by placing a few sticks in the ground and covering them with a roof of boughs or grass. The basic principle of cruck-house building was the method of supping the roof ridge-pole between two or more slanting pairs of posts, " crucks " where they joined one another at the apex. Each cruck was slightly curved and usually consisted of a roughly sawn or adzed tree trunk (generally oak), the ridge-pole being, as a rule, a thinner trunk or a long straight limb. On this simple structure of five pieces of timber the house was built. The spaces between the crucks, both longitudinally and at the gable ends, were filled with some simple walling material supported on subsidiary timber-framing which was sometimes used to strengthen the building and sometimes to make a pleasing pattern.

In the earlier examples the walling material often consisted of a framework of wattle and daub but in later specimens the walls were usually of lath and plaster or brickwork. Some of the larger examples of cruck-houses are two-storeyed dwellings, the upper portion often being lighted by dormer windows in the thatched roof.

CHAPTER VII

WATERMILLS AND WINDMILLS

WATERMILLS

" See you our little mill that clacks
So busy by the brook ?
She has ground her corn and paid her tax
Ever since Domesday Book ! "
KIPLING : " Puck's Song."

Throughout England, scarcely a river or rippling stream flows uninterrupted from source to mouth, for somewhere on its course, sometimes only here and there, sometimes at frequent intervals, an old watermill takes its toll of power from the stream ; a form of power so old that neither record nor tradition tells of its beginning. It is difficult for us, living in an age of mechanical power, to realise that the mother of all modern mechanical marvels was the humble watermill.

It is generally agreed that Greece was the home of the first known watermill ; but the date of its invention and the name of the inventor are unknown. The first allusion to a watermill is found in the celebrated epigram of Antipater of Thessalonica, who flourished about 85 B.C. An early watermill is mentioned by Strabo as belonging to Mithridates, King of Pontus in Asia, who established at Cabira, a contrivance which it has been agreed was a watermill.

These early Greek mills were of very simple construction and exceedingly small in size. Similar mills apparently existed in other parts of Europe for nearly a thousand years. They were ultimately superseded by vastly improved structures of Roman design.

No traces have been found in this country of a Roman watermill, although a number of our old mills still retain pieces of Saxon workmanship and many are mentioned in Domesday Book. Few remaining structures are more than three hundred years old, but several existing mills occupy

AN OLD WATERMILL.

DOMESDAY BOOK REFERENCE TO BARCOMBE MILL.

the sites of earlier ones, erected about a thousand years ago. There is one such mill on the seashore at Bosham, in Sussex, and another, whose history goes back well before the Norman Conquest, is the Barcombe Mill. The fact that mills were working at this spot on the Sussex Ouse is definitely established by the reference in Domesday Book reproduced above :

Translation of the Domesday Book Passage.—" William de Watevile holds of William Bercham (Barcombe) Azor held it of Earl Godwin. Then it was assessed for 13 hides ; now for 10½ hides ; the others are in the rape of the Count of Mortain. They have never paid geld so (the jurors) say. There is land for 20 ploughs. On the demesne are 2 ploughs, and (there are) 24 villeins and 2 bordars with 9 ploughs. There (is) a church, and 3½ miles yielding (de) 20 shillings. In Lewes (are) 18 haws yielding (de) 8 shillings and 7 pence. In the time of King Edward it was worth 12 pounds, and afterwards 6 pounds ; now 8 pounds.''

But the most interesting and picturesque of all the Domesday mills which yet remain is probably Guy's Cliffe corn mill, a mile or two north of Warwick. This mill claims to be one of the oldest existing to-day, and its weatherbeaten stone walls date in part from Saxon times.

There are several types of water-wheels which are still in use ; the undershot, the overshot, the breast, etc.—terms which more or less denote the part of the wheel on which the mill-race impinges. The huge wheels of the undershot

THE WAYFARER'S BOOK

type, i.e. a wheel where the effective head of water is below
the level of the centre, are usually to be found on the more
sluggish streams where the radiating paddles simply dip
into the water like the paddles of a steamer, the wheel being
slowly turned by the impulse of the stream. To make this
more efficient, the portion of the periphery of the wheel
between the point of impact of the water and a position
directly below the centre is usually surrounded by a casing,
generally of stone, which forms a trough that fits closely
enough to the wheel to prevent any considerable escape
of water. A sluice gate is also often placed in front of the
wheel to help increase the power.

The overshot waterwheel, as its name implies, is intended
to be used below falling water and is built in such a position
as to receive its water at the top by means of a small aqueduct
of stone slabs or a wooden trough. These wheels, instead
of straight paddles have curved or kneed buckets, according
to whether they are made of iron plate or of wood, and are
of such a shape as to retain the water down to the lowest
possible point. This type of watermill is usually the most
picturesque form, often being situated in rocky glens amid
lovely scenery.

This direct type of overshot wheel has the water run,
without changing its direction, right over the top, an arrangement which has the advantage that, as the top of the wheel
moves in the same direction as the stream, it gets the benefit
of the whole initial velocity and impulse of the water. On
the other hand, the bottom of the wheel, if at all immersed
in water (which it generally is to some extent) meets with
obstruction by moving against the current.

The pitch-back overshot wheel is a modification of the
latter. This type of waterwheel requires a longer and more
complicated trough which carries the water alongside the
wheel and turns it in a contrary direction before discharging
it on to the top of the wheel. By this change of direction,
part of the impulse from the water is lost but as the bottom
of the wheel moves in the direction of the tail-water it is not
impeded by being immersed in it.

Another, and not very successful form is the breast
waterwheel, which is partly enclosed in a culvert. In such
a type the water is let on to the wheel over the top of a sluice
and is generally applied to the buckets at about 30 degrees
from the top of the wheel. It is an attempt to combine the

action of impulse and gravity, but as much of the water is wasted by passing over the culvert without acting on the buckets this type of waterwheel is only suitable in positions where there is a plentiful supply, but not much fall.

The structure of the overshot and breast wheels is nearly the same as that of the undershot, excepting in the substitution of curved buckets or angled buckets, for straight paddles; but even in the undershot wheel the paddles are sometimes made with a slight curvature.

In any form of waterwheel, the motion may be taken off the axle by torsion, as in Figs. 1 and 3, which necessarily requires rigidity in the arms, or it can be taken directly off

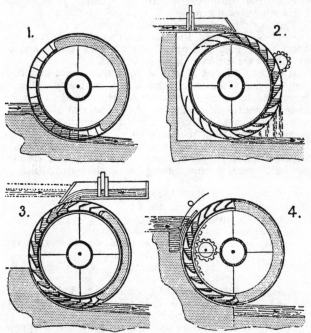

WATERWHEELS: 1. UNDERSHOT.   2. OVERSHOT.   3. PITCH-
BACK OVERSHOT.   4. BREAST.

the periphery, when the power is applied to a pinion working into segments, either external or internal, attached to the shrouding, as in Figs. 2 and 4. In this arrangement, there is no torsion of the axle or strain on the arms, and therefore the wheels are not so massive as the former type.

Almost unnoticed, the watermills, which through countless ages were man's only source of power, are gradually dying out, and every opportunity should be taken of examining any that you may come across during your wanderings, before these great paddle wheels of the streams become— as many another device and custom crushed by progress— just memories.

Note.

Since the above was written the old mill at Barcombe has been burnt down.

The building, which spans the river Ouse, was about one hundred years old, and was constructed largely of timber. Some years ago, it was turned into a button factory and its loss threw some fifty people out of work.

It was at 2 a.m. on March 10, 1939, that flames were seen leaping from the centre of the factory, and before the fire brigade could do anything the whole place was like a furnace. Large quantities of materials and the contents of the office safe were fortunately salvaged ; but although the firemen pumped water from the river on to the flames for seven hours and prevented them from reaching some neighbouring farm buildings, it was a hopeless task to try and save the old mill, which is now nothing but a blackened shell.

OUR WINDMILLS

" Behold, a giant am I !
Aloft here in my tower,
With my granite jaws I devour
The maize, and the wheat, and the rye,
And grind them into flour."
LONGFELLOW, " The Windmill."

Among all the survivals of bygone England to be seen as we wander through the countryside there is none more quaint and picturesque than a windmill.

It stands gaunt against the sky line, primitive in appearance, and if its great sweeps are revolving, suggests some living creature flapping its wings in the air. It carries us

A TOWER WINDMILL.

back, moreover, to one of man's earliest attempts at mechanisation, for the windmill and the watermill were his first successful efforts to harness the forces of nature in his service.

To-day there are other sources of power, so that unfortunately few of these picturesque old structures are working in this country, but if you are fortunate you may still see the great sweeps turning for here and there some old miller clings to the ways of his ancestors, and scorning the assistance of steam or petrol, trusts to the wind to grind his corn.

When windmills were first introduced into England and the country from which they came are facts that cannot be definitely ascertained. Some antiquarians are inclined to think that they came from the near East, for there is a tradition that the Crusaders were the first to introduce the idea to Western Europe. At any rate, there is no evidence that windmills existed before the time of the Crusades. Domesday Book mentions a large number of mills, but in default of any other description it seems probable that they were cattle-mills or watermills, as the windmill, which is known to be a much later invention than either of the other two, would almost certainly have been a sufficient novelty to be specifically mentioned in such a detailed survey.

Several indefinite references in other ancient manuscripts have, however, been found which suggest that windmills were in existence somewhere about the year 1180 but the earliest authentic reference to this type of mill in England is to be found in the " Chronicles of Jocelyn de Brakeload," which describe the building of one by Dean Herbert on his glebe lands at Bury St. Edmunds about 1191.

Unfortunately, the mediæval writers seem entirely to have omitted any description of the appearance of these early windmills, but they have left us several little pictures of them in their manuscripts which enable us to visualise what these mills really looked like. One of these illustrations, an excellent coloured representation occurs on the first page of a Psalter illustrated in the latter half of the thirteenth century, probably about 1270. At one time it was in the possession of William Morris, but is now owned by Mr. Pierpont Morgan. He lent the Psalter to the Exhibition of English Mediæval Art, which was held recently at the Victoria and Albert Museum. The windmill in the illustration is small, but it is quite unmistakably a post mill on a tripod with the usual four sails and tailpost.

The only other thirteenth-century illustration of this type of mill is in Aristotle's *Physica*.   This is in the collection of MSS at the British Museum.

Other pictures of early windmills are to be seen in several of our churches ; but what is probably the best of all these early windmill illustrations is the one in the Louterell Psalter executed for Sir Geoffrey de Louterell about 1340.

Another old picture of a windmill in England is to be found on a memorial brass to Adam de Walsoken, who died in 1349, and can be seen in St. Margaret's Church, King's Lynn, Norfolk.

All these ancient windmills were undoubtedly built of wood for no trace of them has survived, indeed the oldest windmill now in existence was probably built less than three hundred years ago.

Windmills vary considerably in appearance and in construction, but the different types are easily recognisable. Until comparatively recent years only two types were commonly used in this country.

The oldest and naturally the most primitive type is known as a peg or post-mill and is so called because the whole of the wooden upper structure carrying sweeps, wind-shaft and machinery, was pivoted on a huge centre post supported by stout timber beams in tripod form.   This arrangement made it necessary for the entire mill to be turned round to bring the sweeps to face the wind, a job that was done by the miller himself pushing on a long tail beam which projected from the back of the mill.

It is this type of mill that is always pictured in the old manuscripts, and although a fine example of this type can still be seen at Brill in Buckinghamshire, it is undoubtedly a great deal bigger than those which appear in the early illustrations.

The next development from these primitive post mills was the turret post mill.   In this type the post was embedded in a turret of brickwork or masonry instead of being supported by a tripod of timber.   This gave a firmer support to the centre post and made it safe for the mills to be built much higher while the turret also afforded storage accommodation for the sacks of grain or meal in a part of the structure which had previously been wasted.

WINDMILLS

As I have already said, these old mills had to be turned to face the wind by the miller himself.   This was hard work ; and also set a limit to the size of the structure.   Some time during the middle of the sixteenth century it occurred to a clever Fleming that it was really a great waste of labour to turn the whole mill, with all its weight of wheels and stones, when it was really only the sweeps that had to be kept in line with the wind.   So he introduced a new type of mill, called the tower-mill.   In this the sails were affixed to a conical cap or gable at the summit of the building so that the body remained fixed and only the cap and sails were turned.   This made it possible for the tower to be built

OLD PEG OR POST MILL AT BRILL, BUCKS.

of stone or bricks and for it to be both loftier and of greater size than the earlier type of mill.

The cap of the early tower mills was turned like the post-mill by means of a long pole, later this method was replaced by toothed gearing worked by an endless rope. This lightened the labour needed to work the mill, but considerable watchfulness on the part of the miller was still needed, for with strong changing winds much damage could easily be done through not turning the cap to the right position soon enough.

But in the middle of the eighteenth century, a Scottish millwright named Andrew Meikle, who also invented the thrashing machine, introduced what is called the " automatic " fan-wheel. This consists in effect of a small windmill with six or more vanes set at right angles to the sails of the mill proper. This fan remains stationary so long as the sails face the wind, but as the wind veers it causes the fan to revolve. As soon as the fan revolves it sets in motion a gear that turns the whole cap until the sails face square into the wind again and the fan ceases to turn.

Fans were also occasionally attached to the tail poles of post-mills and probably saved many of them from being destroyed, after the improved towermills had been invented.

Several other improvements were introduced during the eighteenth century. In 1772, Meikle invented what is known as the spring sail. Before that date all sails were " common sails," consisting of a framework on which sail-cloth was spread. Each sail had to be set or shortened separately by hand—an unpleasant and difficult job in wet or cold weather or in a strong wind. It was also an operation which, of course, necessitated stopping the mill.

The spring sail consisted of shutters of wood, hinged at one edge and connected together through small cranks to a common sail rod, so that each sail opened and shut rather like a Venetian blind.

To this rod was attached a spring, the tension of which could be varied so that at a given wind pressure the shutters would open and " spill the wind," thus preventing the mill from running away. Although these sails were a definite advance on the common sails, they still suffered from the fact that it was necessary to stop the mill to make the independent adjustment of the sails.

To overcome the disadvantage of this separate adjustment

of the sails, Mr. (afterwards, Sir) William Cubitt, in 1807, invented his " patent sail," in which the sail rods were all connected to one called the striking rod which passed through a hole drilled in the windshaft ; which, as we have seen, carries the sails and is like a great axle. With various gears and couplings, chains and weights, the shutters are automatically controlled and adjusted by a single operation while the mill is still in motion.

Other varieties of sails have been used from time to time. In one type small canvas roller blinds take the place of the wooden shutters of the patent sail.

Another improvement introduced about this time was a brake, to prevent the mill " running away " in a gale, for during high winds cases have occurred in which mills have caught fire through the friction set up by the racing stones.

A slight variant of the towermill is the frock or smock mill. In this form the tower, which is often octagonal in shape, is partially or wholly covered with woodwork, giving an effect as if the tower had a loose smock hung over it. The weather boards are so arranged that each overlaps the one below to throw off rain. There are several theories as to why these mills are so called, the most common being that their appearance resembled a man wearing an old-fashioned smock-frock, but the idea seems rather fantastic.

Smock mills are said to be of Dutch origin and are occasionally spoken of as " Dutch " mills.

CHAPTER VIII

SPORTS AND PASTIMES

HAWKING AND FALCONRY

" My falcon now is sharp, and passing empty ;
    And till she stoop, she must not be full-gorg'd,
    For then she never looks upon her lure."
                                                "Taming of the Shrew."

Falconry, or the art of training and flying hawks for the
purpose of catching other birds, is one of the oldest and most
universal of sports and is, even to-day, occasionally practised
in this country. In ancient times this sport was called
Hawking, a term still preserved in many places, and one
which is, perhaps, more strictly correct.

Hawking has been traced back, as an Eastern sport, to a
period long before the Christian era. It was known in
China about 2000 B.C. and played an important part in the
early history of Persia and India, where it is still eagerly
followed. In Central Europe it seems to have been practised
long before it became established in Great Britain, having
been mentioned by Aristotle and Pliny. It was not until
Saxon times that we find any record of the sport having
been practised in Great Britain. In various illustrated
manuscripts of the period now in the possession of the
British Museum, the sport of hawking is depicted, while
in the celebrated Bayeux tapestry, King Harold is figured
with a hawk upon his wrist. After the Norman Conquest,
however, the interest in the sport of hawking seems to have
made rapid strides, being much indulged in by kings,
nobles and ladies.

In those days the rank of the individual was indicated by
the particular species of hawk he carried. The King alone
was entitled to use the gyrfalcon, a peregrine falcon denoted
an earl, a merlin was the mark of a lady, a goshawk for a
yeoman, a kestrel for a knave, and so on.

FOOT EQUIPMENT, SHOWING HOW JESSES, BELLS AND LEASH ARE ATTACHED.

Always a royal and aristocratic pursuit, hawking was probably at the height of its popularity during the reign of Queen Elizabeth and has possibly done more to make the English a race of true sportsmen than all the rest of our pastimes put together.

In England, the heron is, and always has been, a favourite object of pursuit, the period of the year best adapted for the sport being the breeding season. When a heron is sighted, a case (a pair) of hawks are unhooded and cast " off " and the chase commences.

The heron, seeing the falcons approach, often disgorges its food to lighten itself, and immediately ascends in the air, while the hawks, eager in pursuit and quicker of wing,

1. DUTCH HOOD.   2. INDIAN HOOD.

speedily make upon it and strive to gain a greater elevation by a series of beautiful gyrations. When one of the hawks succeeds in rising above the heron, it stoops, that is, descends swiftly, and in a direct line, upon the game, aiming a stroke with its outstretched legs and talons, at the bird's body. This the heron often succeeds at first in eluding, by a rapid and sudden movement aside. The second hawk, which by this time has also soared, then stoops, while the first is regaining its former altitude, and so on for many successive times, till one hawk at length clutches the heron or binds, upon which her companion joins her, and the three, buoyant by the motion of their wings, descend gently to earth. The falconer's imperative duty is now to be up, or near the spot where the three birds are descending, to divert the attention of the hawks before they reach the ground, and entice them from the quarry to him by means of the lure. This is very necessary, as the heron is extremely dangerous, and has been frequently known to injure the hawks with its sharp beak when on the ground, though it is all but harmless while in the air, for there is no truth in the idea that the heron, as a means of defence, sometimes impales the descending enemy upon its beak. When the heron's wounds have been dressed—for this bird is rarely killed in such encounters—a ring with the captor's name is usually affixed to its leg, after which it is set at liberty, and so becomes available for future sport. The gyrfalcon was the bird generally used for this sport later on, but modern falconers seem unable to adapt these northern hawks to present conditions and depend almost wholly upon our native peregrine. In the fourteenth century, however, a gyrfalcon was considered the only bird fit to attack the stately heron and a gift of such a lordly hawk was indeed a kingly offering, and was frequently employed when the good will of a near or distant potentate was particularly desired.

By the early twentieth century the " Noble Art " was almost extinct in England, but the Old Hawking Club (until 1925) and the British Falconers' Club from that date, still forms a nucleus for the few enthusiasts who practise the sport.

There are two different types of hawks which are suitable for this sport. First are the long-winged, high-flying hawks, which include the Iceland and Greenland gyrfalcon already mentioned, and the peregrine. These birds are usually termed "hawks of the lure." Secondly come the short-winged, fast, low-flying, hawks which include the goshawk and sparrowhawk, these being termed "hawks of the fist." No quarry is better suited to the capacities of the peregrine, or "gentle falcon," than the Scotch red grouse. But the "gentle" part is forgotten when the hawk makes its thunderbolt assault, diving on its victim from a height or "pitch" of hundreds of feet, usually killing it clean with a single resounding blow of the half-closed fist.

Unlike the true falcons, the short-winged goshawk hunts on or near the ground and trusses (holds) to its victim till the latter ceases to struggle, no matter how fierce and rough the tussle may be. It kills by the vice-like squeeze of its piercing talons, instead of by the terrific blow of the half-open foot, as do the true falcons. These hawks are the fiercest and most competent killers of all and were therefore used principally by the "yeomanry" as meat getters.

Although too small and slight for "regular" game, the sparrowhawk is uncommonly fierce and courageous, and

FALCON HOODED AND RESTING ON BLOCK.

makes spirited dashes at such quarry as starlings and black-birds. It is a hedgerow hunter, depending for success upon the intrepidity of its onslaught and the pertinacity with which it follows its victim. It will even run through thick cover after skulking quarry.

The training of hawks, which should commence when they are just fledged but have not left the nest, is a difficult process, requiring much skill and discretion ; consequently in olden times the office of falconer was a post of considerable importance. For certain purposes the male or " tiercel "* is considered superior, but as a rule the " falcon " the name usually applied to the female, is much more highly esteemed for sporting purposes, being larger and more powerful.

The process of training hawks has been discussed by numerous authors in many books and in various languages, but whatever method is employed, the object is always the same, and that is to teach the birds to be obedient. The several implements used in the training are the hood, jesses, bells, the lure, block and the cadge. The hood is a cap of leather and is the principal means by which a hawk is controlled, but its use is often a little misunderstood. The bird is not kept blindfolded nearly all the time but, on the contrary, is hooded only when there is a possibility of its being unnecessarily disturbed while undergoing training, and a bird once thoroughly accustomed to wearing it can be taken anywhere and handled quite easily. After the training is completed, the hood is used to prevent the bird from starting off after undesirable game.

During the early part of the training the jesses and bells are attached and become permanent fixtures even during the birds' flights. Jesses are two short strips of leather placed round the hawk's legs, to which the leash, by which the bird is held, is attached. The little metal bells are affixed, one to each leg, just above the jess, and are of great assistance in locating the hawk when the quarry has been killed out of sight.

The lure is generally a bunch of feathers attached to a cord, in the centre of which is usually a piece of spliced wood, to which a portion of meat can be attached. By

---

* The term tiercel is derived from the Latin *tertius*, according to some because every third bird in the nest is supposed to be a male ; according to others because the male is supposed to be a third smaller than the female.

accustoming the hawk to feed off the lure, or to come to it at a certain call or whistle to be fed when on the wing, the lure becomes an important part of the falconer's equipment and by it he is enabled to entice his bird back after the chase. On such occasions the falconer reclaims his bird by swinging the baited lure round and round his head, accompanying the action by some well-known call.

Blocks are portions of tree trunks firmly fixed in the ground, upon which the hawks sit when at rest and to which they are secured by the leash. The cadge consists of four pieces of wood, padded and fixed together in the form of an oblong frame, on which the birds perch when being carried from one place to another. Transverse straps enable it to be hung over the falconer's shoulders so that the hawks sit all round him.

To ensure success with hawks one should always resolve to keep before him the two major maxims of the falconer, *gentleness* and *patience*, because he must have the former and he will need plenty of the latter ; but with due care and, above all, plenty of exercise, a hawk may be kept as long as twenty years, being active as a sporting bird the whole of that time. Many hawks will be found to develop an extremely affectionate disposition towards their masters.

ARCHERY

Archery is the art and practice of shooting with the bow and arrow, an art which can undoubtedly lay claim to a greater antiquity than falconry. The origin is, in fact, lost in the uncertainties of prehistoric times, and we have no means of ascertaining when and how man first discovered the principle of these weapons. Flint arrow heads, which

PRACTICE WITH THE LONG BOW IN THE TIME OF EDWARD III, AFTER THE LUTTRELL PSALTER (VETUSTA MONUMENT).

have been found in great numbers, date back, according to different anthropologists, from 25,000 to 50,000 years; and in all probability arrows without stone points were used for unknown ages before that.

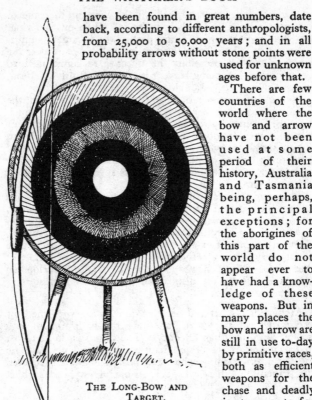

THE LONG-BOW AND
TARGET.

There are few countries of the world where the bow and arrow have not been used at some period of their history, Australia and Tasmania being, perhaps, the principal exceptions; for the aborigines of this part of the world do not appear ever to have had a knowledge of these weapons. But in many places the bow and arrow are still in use to-day by primitive races, both as efficient weapons for the chase and deadly instruments for war. From the very earliest times these simple weapons, of one type or another, have been used by the great military nations, such as the Greeks, Assyrians, Hindus, Turks, Chinese and English, and have been a potent factor in establishing their power.

In England the highest development of military archery was reached between the early part of the fourteenth and the latter part of the fifteenth century, when the English archers became the most celebrated infantry in Europe and their skill was the deciding factor at such battles as Crecy, Poitiers and Agincourt during the Hundred Years War with France ; and again at the time of the Wars of the Roses when, to a great extent, they decided the fate of the day on several battlefields in England.

This little book is no place for a lengthy discussion on the many types of bows and arrows used in this ancient art. It is sufficient to note that the two principal classifications are based on form and mechanism and are known as :

(1) Free Bows,   (2) Crossbows.

The free bow is the ordinary stave-and-string bow, the crossbow, or Arbalest, on the other hand, has its bow-stave attached transversely to a stem or stock, which has a notch to hold back the string when the bow is bent, and some form of releasing device or trigger.

The crossbow was much in use during feudal times, and continued to be a favoured weapon in England up to the end of the thirteenth century. It was at the battle of Falkirk, in 1298, that the long-bow definitely established its supremacy, it being found that an archer armed with this type of bow could discharge a dozen arrows during the time that the arbalester was winding-up his cumbrous crossbow and discharging one.

Some considerable time after the discovery of gunpowder, archery was still in use for military purposes ; but with the gradual improvement in the effectiveness of firearms, it was eventually abandoned, the forces of Elizabeth being the last in which it played any important role. We may regard the Honourable Artillery Company, the oldest military body in the kingdom, as the last survival, or rather imago, of a regiment of English archers. This corps was formed in 1537, during the reign of Henry VIII, under the title of the Guild or Fraternity of St. George, and from it were always selected the officers of the City Trained Bands.

Although discontinued for military purposes, archery was still widely enjoyed as a sport.

Towards the end of the eighteenth century the formation of the Royal Toxophilite Society of London and the participation in the sport by the then Prince of Wales, revived and established modern archery as we know it. To-day, this Society is recognised as the controlling authority in the sport.

In 1844 the Grand National Meeting, which, ever since, has determined the championships of England, was held for the first time, and standards and rules adopted.

In Scotland archery is splendidly upheld by the Royal Company of Archers at Edinburgh, who still practise archery as a pastime, and compete annually for a silver arrow bearing the date 1603, which, with a number of other threads of continuity that can be followed, forms a connecting link between ancient and modern bowmanship. The recorded minutes of the society date from 1676.

This Royal Company of Archers lays claim by Royal Charter to the curious privilege of acting as the bodyguard of the reigning sovereign whenever he, or she, approaches within five miles of the city of Edinburgh.

The equipment for modern archery consists of a bow, with its string, arrows, finger-tips or shooting glove, a bracer or arm-guard, a quiver, and a target.

The standard English bow is divided by a handle, of plush or leather, into upper and lower limbs. These taper gradually and are nearly flat on the back and half round on the face. Nocks are usually cut near the ends to receive the string ; or curved tips of horn, also nocked, are added.

Bows, if made of one piece of wood, are termed " self," but if composed of two or more strips of wood glued together they are described as " backed." The former are invariably made of yew, the latter of various combinations.

The length of a man's bow should be about six feet, that of a woman, five feet six inches. The strength of a bow is reckoned by the number of pounds it requires to pull it a distance (from string to bow when fully bent) of twenty-eight inches in the case of a man's, and twenty-five inches in that of a woman's.

The parts of an arrow are the shaft, tip, feathers and nock. The woods most often used are spruce or Norway pine. A self-arrow, like a self-bow, is one made of a single piece of wood, while a footed-arrow has a piece of hardwood spliced on to the tip to improve its flight and give it strength.

The shooting glove and bracer are made of leather and are used to protect the arm and fingers from being hurt by the string when shooting.

The standard target is four feet in diameter and is usually made of straw rope, tightly compressed and sewn into a spiral. On the canvas face which covers it is painted a central gold spot or bulls-eye, around which is a red ring. Then follows a ring of blue ; a black ring surrounds this and outside of all is a white ring bordered with green.

Chapter IX

WORK IN THE COUNTRY

SHEPHERDS AND SHEEP

To many people a shepherd's calling may seem at first sight a leisurely one, compared with that of some of the other farm hands ; but it is by no means so in fact. Quite apart from his anxious and sleepless nights during the lambing season, his daily work of folding is a heavier task than most labourers will willingly undertake.

A good shepherd is generally the most independent of the farmer's servants, jealous of his skill and reticent to a degree.

It was from a Sussex shepherd acquaintance, a grand, weather-beaten old man of seventy-two years, who has been tending the flocks there for sixty summers, that I learned much about sheep. I first met him late one evening at the beginning of the lambing season several years ago. At the time he was busy converting a mountain of straw faggots, hurdles, stakes and wire into a neat lambing yard and during the days that followed I realised the full meaning of the laconic term " good " as applied to shepherding.

All through those cold days and nights, Shepherd George, as I will call him, attended unceasingly, without tiring, to his sheep, ever alert for signs of uneasiness, never failing to distinguish between ordinary " mobbing " and " trouble " in the voice of his charges.

Quick to ease a ewe in difficulties and to carry the youngster to the warmth of the yard, his grey eyes twinkling with pleasure and kindness, yet he never interfered if necessity did not demand his aid.

One of a shepherd's great hopes during the lambing season is to find a jet-black lamb among his flock. For although this little chap, so conspicuous among his fellows, is invariably nicknamed " The Devil," he is always regarded as a mascot which will bring good luck for the rest of the season.

During the rain, frost and wind of winter, when ploughs have stopped and other men have been driven to barns to dress corn or to idleness in their cottages, the whack, whack of a crowbar on stake heads is still heard. The shepherd will be setting to-morrow's pen—that is, moving and setting up hurdles in a field in which the sheep are being fed. This problem of feeding is usually solved by what is known as " spring keep "—acres and acres of clover, sainfoin and vetches, grown specially for the sheep in some fairly sheltered part of the downs.

On closer inspection these " spring keeps " prove to be wide fields of scented flowers, where rose-pink heads of sainfoin mingle in the wildest confusion with white and Dutch clover. But to the old shepherd it is all so many days' " keep." Last of these crops is the Dutch grattans or aftermath clover. After these are exhausted he moves his flock to the tares.

In summer, Old George tends his sheep among the whins on the downs, where they have fared so well on the close-cropped turf from time immemorial.

There are many, many other jobs with which the shepherd has to contend, such as docking, dipping and shearing.

A short time ago some dear old lady wrote to the papers protesting against what she called the cruel practice of docking, or cutting short, the tails of young lambs. It was very clear that she did not understand what she was talking about. Far from being a cruel practice, docking, in the case of sheep, is a real kindness. The cutting short of lambs' tails has been practised for centuries and is necessary for cleanliness. The tail of a sheep is too short and too heavy to be of much use to it ; but it is long enough to cause the hindquarters of the animal to become very dirty. If filth is allowed to stay on the wool, it attracts the blow-fly, which lays its eggs on the sheep. Soon these eggs hatch out into small maggots, which at once begin to feed on the flesh of the sheep, causing much pain and irritation. A sheep which has been " struck " does not thrive and if not attended to it will creep away to a shady place and die. If the tail is docked there is less wool for dirt to stick to · and the actual docking causes little or no pain, the lamb having very little sense of feeling in its tail at that early age. A wedge-shaped, sharp iron, at a dull heat, is used for the job, the tail being severed at a joint, the heat simultaneously cauterising the wound. A soothing ointment is also applied.

Sheep (like human beings) are subject to a number of diseases, one of the most unpleasant of which is known as sheep-scab. This is caused by a minute parasite, about the size of a cheese mite. It burrows beneath the skin, setting up excessive irritation, so that the sheep rubs itself against hurdles and posts and damages its wool. The best, in fact the only way to prevent this disease is to dip the animals in a solution composed principally of sulphur, quicklime and water. In some places the sheep are lowered into the dip in a sort of cage, but the old dipping-troughs are still used in many districts. They are made of stout planks, with a sloped draining-board at one end on which the sheep must stand for a minute or more after clambering out of the dip, to let as much as possible of

SHEEP DIPPING.

THE WAYFARER'S BOOK

the precious liquid run back. Otherwise the bath would be quickly emptied, as their fleeces act like so many sponges.

By the laws of England this dipping must be done at least once a year, and the bath must last at least a minute, every sheep being completely submerged in the dip, all except its head ; for they must not swallow any, because some of the dips are poisonous. A tool, sometimes called a paddle, which consists of a piece of wood or strip of hoop-iron fitted to a long handle, is often used to help in submerging the animals. As the sheep swim through the dip the shepherd, or one of his helpers standing at the side of the trough, plants the tool firmly on the middle of the animal's back and relentlessly pushes it under. That dipping is a good thing is proved by the fact that sheep-scab occurs but rarely in England nowadays.

HOPS AND HOPPING

If your wanderings take you into the hop-growing districts of Kent, you cannot fail to notice the quaint brick buildings that are scattered over the countryside very like giant candle-extinguishers. They look like structures built to stand for centuries and will undoubtedly outlast many a modern building. Sometimes there is but one in a hop-garden, often two, occasionally three and on large estates six or eight peep above the bines and orchards. They are what are known as Oast-houses. Oast is a word meaning *kiln*, and these quaint buildings are the kiln-houses in which the hops are dried.

Kent is not the only county in which you will find hop gardens and oast-houses. True they are more numerous and the gardens far more extensive than in other counties, but Sussex, Surrey, Hampshire, Herefordshire and Worcestershire all have large areas of fertile land for the cultivation of hops. In the last named county the gardens are usually spoken of as yards.

There is considerable variety in the design of oast-houses, but they are easily recognised by their conical roofs and white painted cowls, with the long, projecting vane that keeps the opening in the cowl turned away from the wind. In Kent, most of the oast-houses are circular in form, a shape that ensures more equal weathering and less resistance to the high winds.

By the way, in Kent, a kiln is always spoken of as a "kell," so remember when next in that county to do likewise.

The hop is first mentioned by Pliny as one of the garden plants of the Romans, who, it appears, ate the young shoots as we eat asparagus; and, in fact, many country people in England do the same at the present day.

Wild hops are native to Britain but they need a warm, sheltered place and much skilled cultivation to grow them for commercial purposes. A number of varieties have been raised during the last century, among the best-known being the Bramling, named after a farm at Lekham near Canterbury, and Fuggle's and Golding's, each named after the grower. Once planted, they live many years, which sounds as if they would be a cheap crop to grow, but it is just the reverse. Hops are the most laborious

THE STILT MAN.

crop to produce; there is something to be done every month in the year; they need a rich soil and then much manuring and hoeing. In winter there are the old bines to clear away and burn and the land to be ploughed and possibly drained; the poles and wires to repair, and so on.

It takes three years for the hops to reach perfection. During their first year of growth the plants add little to their height or to the number and strength of their bines. The third year they reach their full height of from fourteen to twenty feet. The size of the plant and the number of its bines are restricted in order to concentrate the energy of the plant on the formation of good fruit, by the removal of bines of very strong or very weak growth. Continual attention is necessary during their growth as hops are a prey to many insect pests, and there has to be much spraying, in which nicotine figures largely. Clouds of sulphur are also blown over the plants as they come into flower, to prevent mildew.

Towards the end of the summer the ripening fruits begin to swell and acquire a scent. Now appear the famous stilt-men, whose difficult art has been handed down from father to son for generations. On stilts eighteen feet high they pick their precarious way between the rows of tall plants, tying the topmost bines to the highest strings.

When the plump and aromatic cones of the female flowers are firm and crisp to the touch and have a beautiful purplish tint, they are ready for picking.

A hop garden in the early autumn is one of the fairest sights of the Garden of England. The bines, trained on countless rows of wires and poles, form exquisite vistas of dark green foliage, broken only by the golden garlands of hops.

Then follows the invasion of the hop-pickers. It is necessary to employ an enormous number, as the hops must be picked directly they are ripe. As most of the hops are quite beyond the reach of even the tallest person, it is one man's job to go round with a bill-hook. This he uses to cut the supporting strings where they are fastened to the overhead wire. The plants immediately collapse into an untidy heap and are quickly stripped of their harvest by the nimble fingers of the pickers.

The pickers are organised into small parties, each party having a bin or a crib assigned to it into which to put the hops as they are picked. A bin is a light structure made of sacking on a rough wooden frame and can easily be moved by two men, as the work progresses from hill to hill, each "hill" being one plant from which four to six bines are trained up the strings and poles.

Bin-men or bushellers go round several times a day collecting the hops. These are measured into pokes, loose yellow sacks holding ten bushels.

Many expressions peculiar to hop growing districts are often heard in the hop gardens, mostly in connection with the work, "The Catch," "Slight," "Heavy," "The Tally," for example.

When a crop is good, the hops are "heavy"; when small the hops are "slight." "The Tally" is not the actual reckoning or total of what is picked, but the rate at which the picker is paid; thus "a shilling for four bushels, or a shilling for five."

Hop-pickers always say "bushels" though the

Hops.

basket in which the hops are measured generally holds much more than a bushel. "The Catch" is an expression used for a "very small bushel"—less than half a basket—and it is sometimes given as a favour with the last measuring on Saturdays.

When the hops have been collected they are carted to the oast-houses. Here men work day and night throughout the whole of the picking season of four, five, or even six weeks.

Once the fires are lighted, drying never stops. This operation requires to be performed with great care.

An old oast-house is usually a two-storeyed building with two or more kilns. On the ground floor is a brazier, burning coke or anthracite and occasionally charcoal. Sulphur is also burnt with the fuel to give a good golden colour to the drying hops. It can be imagined what the atmosphere in the oast-house is like, for in it the men must work for several weeks to tend the fires.

On the upper floor, doors open into the kilns and the hops are spread evenly a foot or eighteen inches deep on hair cloths on wooden slats so that the hot air can rise freely through them. Drying takes about eleven hours, during which period the hops are turned many times with barn-shovels. Drying is complete when the hops are quite brittle. At the exact moment they are raked out and a fresh layer spread in the kiln.

For a few days the dried hops lie about in heaps to cool and when ready are pushed with a " scippet "—a light, wooden shovel, two or more feet wide—into a hole in the floor from which hangs a bag or pocket eight feet long. Into this they are pressed, generally with a ram or plunger worked by a winch. Not so many years ago a boy was employed to do this job by treading the hops. Each full pocket holds just over a hundredweight and a half, and when stuffed tight it is as hard as a block of wood. As each one is filled it is lowered to the ground floor after being roughly tied up and in due course it is neatly sewn up and weighed. The pockets are then marked with the grower's name and the year and the kind of hops they contain.

They are then ready for market and are sent straight to London or to some local town, such as Maidstone, Hereford or Worcester, to await a purchaser.

A Typical Kentish Oast-House.

WORK IN THE COUNTRY

HAYMAKING

Although there are many excellent foods produced by scientific methods for the winter feeding of cattle, even the best of them are unable to take the place of the bulk food provided by good sundried fodder.

With the coming of midsummer, haymaking gets into full swing. Green grass is cut and made into the hay without which no stock-keeper can carry on. A generation ago, scythes, rakes and picks (pitchforks) were the only tools used in making hay, but during the last twenty years, more and more machines, increasingly formidable, have invaded the hayfields. These modern methods have done a great deal to facilitate the work but have robbed haymaking of much of its glamour and turned the immensely laborious, deliberate ritual that it used to be, into a noisy, dusty job to be got over as quickly as possible. In the days of the scythe the haysel occupied two or three months on a large farm ; now the same number of weeks will often suffice in good weather.

The uninitiated often think that sunshine is necessary to the successful making of hay. This is not so, for sun can often spoil hay more surely than rain. Bright, dry, breezy weather is really the best haymaker.

Before the coming of machinery, " making " the hay took three or four days. Very early on the first day the grass was cut by men with scythes. The leading man started by cutting a swath straight along the side of the field, the next following him cutting the next swath, and so on as it were in steps. The swaths were cut in one direction right across the field and back, not round and round as a reaping-machine cuts it. Next, about nine o'clock when the sun was beginning to make itself felt, the swaths were thrown about or " tedded " by the pitchfork wielders, so that the wind could blow through them ; thus the grass was thoroughly spread and partly dried. In the evening of the same day it was raked together as neatly as possible, in small heaps, called " pooks " or " haycocks," so that the dews or possible rain at night should not penetrate.

On the second day, if the weather was clear in the morning and likely to remain fine for the day, the hay was again scattered over the ground, not spread thinly but covering about half the field. It was turned and tossed again and again so as to dry it evenly and get it into as good a condition as possible. When the hay was fit to carry, it was " spurred in " to a " windrow " and thence loaded into the wagons to be carried away to barns or to be stacked by skilled men at the homestead. With the invention of machinery for performing practically all these operations the whine of the tractor has largely replaced the merry shouts of the children and chatter of the women and robbed the haysel of much of its romance.

There are several different grades of hay. The first to be cut is sainfoin, which makes the hard, brown hay so prized by racehorse trainers. Clover and rye-grass are the next to be mown—a crop of temporary leys giving the sweet-smelling " mixture " used for horses and fattening cattle. Then comes the harvesting of meadow grass, the hay from which forms the basis of cows' rations during the winter. The rough pastures and downlands are then shorn to keep the cattle and outlying stock when the days are short and no grass is growing.

Why Haystacks Heat

One occasionally hears or reads accounts in the newspapers of haystacks being deliberately set on fire by some evil-minded person or by some careless individual throwing away a lighted cigarette end, but it is not often realised that the fire is sometimes created by the stack itself.

It is quite a common thing for haystacks to get " warm " a short time after being built, and sometimes they become so hot as to burst into flames. No satisfactory explanation has yet been discovered as to what actually causes the hay to ignite, but it is known that bacteria and fungi have a hand in causing the temperature at first.

If the hay is a bit too wet when carried, it sinks and binds together so tightly that any heat formed cannot escape quickly. The grasses or clover " sweat " and bacteria become active. This means that heat is being given off, and the warmer it gets the faster do the bacteria work, and the faster they work the more heat they produce. At last the heat gets too great even for bacteria, but soon a certain amount of charring takes place.

It is thought that the charred material is in so fine a state that gases condense upon its surface so rapidly as to produce flames, and the hay starts to burn, and once a stack is on fire it is almost impossible to save it or control the flames

BUILDING A HAYSTACK.

before most of the hay is destroyed. A hay farmer is always on the watch once the stacks are built and often cuts a hole into the stack to enable any heat to escape and so prevent the possibility of a fire.

Tonning the Hay

It is a highly skilled job to build a stack of hay, and an equally skilled one to gauge, from the outside, its exact size, density and weight after it is built. As hay is usually bought and sold in the stack the art of estimating its weight in tons, or " Tonning the Hay " as it is called, is a tricky and difficult business.

So much depends on the way in which a stack has been built. For instance, two ricks of meadow hay may be exactly the same size and age, and yet one may weigh 30 per cent more than the other. This disparity in weight is due largely to the difference in solidity and quality, the hay in the heavy rick having set much tighter than that in the lighter one. This, again, is due mainly to the amount of heat generated.

For thirty days after stacking, the hay settles considerably. A tall stack may lose as much as three feet of height. After the first month the settling is slower, but it often continues throughout the life of a stack.

The unit commonly used for estimating the tonnage of a rectangular stack is the truss which contains 56 pounds of hay. The plane measurements of a truss are three feet by two feet, but the depth varies between twelve and eighteen inches according to density.

To find the volume of a rectangular rick, with gable roof, measurements of the length, width and height are multiplied together. The height is taken from the base to the eaves of the thatch, plus one-third of the distance from the eaves to the ridge.

It is a simple matter to calculate the number of " plane " trusses in a rectangular stack. If the base of the stack measures 30 feet by 20 feet, then it contains one hundred " plane " trusses. It only remains to agree upon a depth for the truss to complete the calculation—at least as far as the eaves.

If a truss depth of eighteen inches is agreed and the stack measures fifteen feet to the eaves, then it is assumed to contain one thousand trusses, or 25 tons of hay. Suppose, however, that the hay is much denser and that the correct depth for a truss is twelve inches : then the stack will actually contain thirty-seven tons of hay. With hay at £5 a ton, this difference in tonnage would result in a cash difference of £60 on one stack alone.

CHAPTER X

SOME ANCIENT COUNTRY CRAFTS

CHARCOAL BURNING

Wayfarers who cling to the by-ways see many quaint sights hidden from the lordly ones who travel by main roads only. Even in these times, when mass production is the order of the day, there are still many queer crafts practised in out-lying places, such, for instance, as charcoal burning. Charcoal was used by the smiths and ironfounders long before the coal of the earth was dreamed of, and the art of making it has altered little since Saxon days.

You may have a little difficulty in finding one of the old craftsmen, for he is becoming a rare bird ; but if your luck is good, and you do discover one, you will have found a man whose occupation is of absorbing interest.

During the winter months the charcoal burner is busy cutting and stacking his piles of wood, and as four tons are needed to produce one ton of charcoal, and many different kinds of wood are required for the various qualities, the winter months are none too long for the preparation of his actual craft.

When the rain storms and winds have passed, and the weather begins to improve, the burner generally carts all the carefully accumulated stacks of wood to some clearing in the forest, where later the " hearths " or " pits " will be built. Then begins the job of sorting and grading the different kinds of wood, a business that requires the greatest care and knowledge. The whole secret of good charcoal is good, even smouldering, and thus it is necessary that all the wood should burn at the same rate.

The sticks are first cut into lengths or billets of about three feet and sorted into thicknesses of one, two and three inches. In building the hearth a stump is driven into the centre of the clearing to serve as an axis round which the pit is built up. Three billets are then laid on the ground

round the stump in such a way as to enclose a triangle, with the ends overlapping. Three others are laid upon the first, three more on the second and so on until they form a triangular chimney some three or more feet high. Next billets are laid in a slightly leaning manner against the chimney, in successive rings, until the pit has reached the required diameter. The thicker billets are placed nearer the centre of the cone, with the thinner ones on the outside. As the length of the billets is the same, a fairly flat top is obtained. On this the upper course is set. A beginning is made by placing shorter billets horizontally and radially round the chimney, like the spokes of a wheel. Succeeding layers are placed so that their inner ends are more and more raised, until, by the time the last ones are placed, they are inclining at a steep angle, which gives the pit rather the appearance of a native hut.

The whole heap, except at the base where a belt is left to admit the air, is then covered with heather or straw, over which earth or ashes are shovelled, damped with water, and beaten down till there are no airholes left. The firing is started by dropping a couple of shovelfuls of red-hot charcoal down the chimney from which the central part has been removed. The hole is then filled with unlighted charcoal and finally sealed with a lump of turf.

The whole burning process usually takes about a week, during which time the charcoal burner lives in a hut close to the fire, for every few hours he has to attend to it, throwing water on the ashes and carefully watching that no holes appear. Only the right amount of air to keep the heat up must be admitted, or the pit will take fire and £20 or £30 worth of damage may be done.

As an extra safeguard, the hearths are also sheltered from the wind by thatched hurdles or " looes " which can be moved round as the wind changes.

Charcoal is still used to some extent as fuel in the Kentish oast-houses, for the purpose of drying the hops, and the best variety for this job is made from alder, which is largely grown in Kent and Sussex. For the steel industry, oak and ash generally produce the best charcoal; lime is also burned and gives the finest material for artists' pencils, while birch, chestnut and beech are used for the making of chemical charcoal. But many other woods are used, even though they may be green.

CHARCOAL BURNING.

" Jove's oak, the warlike ash, vein'd elm, the softer buck,
   Short hazel, maple plain, light asp, the bending wych,
   Tough holly, and smooth birch, may altogether burn."

STRIPPING THE GIANTS

Any day, in late April, or in May, a familiar sight on many
a country road is a wagon or lorry, piled high with layers of
oak bark, on its way to the nearest tanner's yard. For
despite all the claims of present-day chemicals, oak-bark,
by virtue of certain rich juices in its sap, still retains its old
value as a means of tanning hides.

The stripping of the bark is best done immediately the
tree has been felled, for every hour that the bark is left on a
thrown tree not only makes it harder to remove but means

deterioration in its value for tanning purposes. For this reason the bark-peelers or flawers work with the tree-fellers and begin their work almost as the tree comes to rest.

The flawers are equipped with sharp, small stripping axes (for the purpose of making an incision into the bark first of all) and a long iron implement called a "flawing-spud," which is something like a screwdriver twenty to thirty inches long, ending in a sharp, wedge-shaped scoop. With this tool great lengths of bark can be ripped off at one sweep.

The flawers start by making their outline cuts, with their axes, half-way round the trunk and some three or four feet along it. Two men usually work together, the one pressing and digging in with his flawing spud, the other helping by wrestling the bark away with his bare hands. They work with unhurried precision in busy silence, broken only by the noise of tools and the sudden sigh of the bark as it comes away with a noise like tearing silk. In an hour or so the tree which has stood in the woods for several centuries, is bare, and the hands of the flawers are stained by the sap a deep, inky blue, the trade-mark of the craft throughout the season.

The bark having been stripped is carefully stacked so that the air can get in to dry and weather it. At first it is lissom and springy, but in time it hardens and stiffens and cracks on pressure. It is then ready for the tanyard. Before the bark can be soaked in the "leaches," as the tan pits are called, it is chopped into pieces about two inches square, and some time elapses before the resulting tannic acid is completely extracted.

THATCHING

One of the most interesting figures in the country, and one you are almost sure to meet during a day's wandering in September, is the thatcher. Hayricks are usually thatched during that month and occasionally you may be lucky enough to see one of these skilled craftsmen at work repairing, or even rebuilding, the roof of some old cottage ; for although many other materials are now used for roofs, thatch still holds its own in many parts of the country.

A few years ago there was a danger of this old craft dying out and rarely more than one or two skilled men were to be found in the same district. Now, however, there seems to be a considerable revival of this ancient calling.

If you do have the good fortune to see a thatcher at work, pause awhile, for his work is extremely interesting to watch.

Thatching is an art that has changed but little in the course of hundreds of years and is a well-paid craft, because the profession is not overcrowded. The tools used for the work are few and simple; most of them are made by the village blacksmith or the thatcher himself and are often handed down from father to son for several generations.

One of these quaint implements that practically every thatcher uses is known as a leggett. This is a flat, wooden mallet with a head about nine inches square, studded with heavy nails. A large knife (often a scythe blade with a short handle), several needles, two or more feet in length, a bill-hook, a steel thatching pin and a small pair of shears, such as are used for sheep-shearing, more or less complete his kit.

Like many other tools and implements used by country folk, those of the thatcher often have local names, a fact which, to a townsman, is rather confusing. To attempt a description of all the various methods and styles of thatching would completely fill a little book of this size for there are dozens of local fashions in most counties, and often individual thatchers have a style of their own.

SINGLE TWIST SPICK. DOUBLE TWIST SPICK.

The material used for the work varies greatly. In Dorset, wheat-straw, locally called reed, is favoured; in Norfolk, river-reed finds first place; in Essex, rushes. In other places, oat-straw from the threshing machines is used, while furze, heather and bracken often give service in moorland and mountain districts. In fact, the material usually chosen is that which is most easily obtainable locally.

For rick thatching straw is probably used more than most other materials, as it is usually only required to last for twelve months or so ; but for the thatching of houses and cottages, river-reed, as used by the Norfolk thatchers, is probably the most lasting ; in fact it has been known to last, with little or no repair, for well over a century.

Another important point about river-reed is that it is much less inflammable than the other materials.

Before straw is fit to be used for thatching it must first be well cleaned. This, like everything else connected with the art, is done in various ways in different districts.

In the Midlands the straw is prepared by the very simple method of straightening it, handful by handful, by drawing it through both hands from the middle of the bundle. The broken straws and weeds are thus pulled out and discarded. This process is known as " yelming " or " gabbling," and the bundles of clean straw are usually known as " yelms." In Devon the straw is also cleaned by hand, but with the help of a comb about a foot wide, with long tines set an inch or more apart. In Sussex, some thatchers use a stick for

THATCHED COTTAGES AT EAST LULWORTH, DORSET.

LARGE QUAINT THATCH AT SELWORTHY, SOMERSET.

the work which is often known as the " duck " ; in other districts a mechanical device is employed ; but many of the older craftsmen say that this method is not as satisfactory as cleaning by hand.

Whatever the method of cleaning employed, however, it is first absolutely essential that the straw is well wetted, for dry straw will never lie close and smooth on a rick or roof—a most important point if the thatch is to remain weatherproof during the rains of the winter months.

A hayrick is never thatched directly it is completed by the haymakers, but is left for several weeks to stand, for it will often lose a foot or more in height before it finally settles down, and the thatcher is able to start his work.

I have already mentioned that individual thatchers have individual ways of working ; but the principal method of thatching a rick is as follows :—

When the yelms are ready a number of them are taken up the ladder, which has been placed against the rick, and are secured to a " spear " or " spike " driven into the hay where it may be most easily reached.

The thatch is started along the eaves. The straw is spread out flat so as to form a horizontal " lane " or " strake "

THE WAYFARER'S BOOK

some two or three inches thick, with the ears pointing upwards and the butts downwards. The straw that projects slightly lower than the eaves is intended finally to remain, and is generally fixed about a foot from the lower end by pegging across it a twist of straw, or twine.

The pegs that the thatcher uses are of several types. Some are single-pointed sticks two feet long on which twine is wound to hold on the thatch. These are generally called thatching spars. The others are known as spicks. These are sticks of split hazel or sallow, which are twisted double and pointed at each end like a large hairpin. The single-twist spick is generally used on ricks, while the double-twist is for house thatching.

Spicks are, as a rule, made during April and May, for at that time of year the newly cut wood is still green enough to be twisted without snapping.

It is very important that the spicks be driven into the hay with their points in a slightly upwards direction, so as to prevent rain running down them into the hay and rotting it. As each handful of yelm is spread out the last one is tapped and raked until it lies evenly before being pegged and fixed.

The first lane being completed, the second is laid so as to lap halfway over the first, the third over the second and so on. The second lane and all those above it are placed with butts uppermost. As each lane is laid it is securely fastened to the rick.

On some ricks, particularly small ones, the thatcher often lays a section of three or four lanes at the same time to save going repeatedly round the rick. When the ridge is reached, the butts of the last two lanes which come together from either side are worked into each other so as to interlock. Some thatchers lay a yelm right over the ridge so as to make a still neater finish, but this is not often thought necessary. When all is securely fastened the eaves are trimmed with the small shears and the gleaming straw " hat " is finished. And although the thatch is only a few inches thick, the skilled thatcher lays it so cleverly that it will keep the rick dry for twelve months or even longer.

House-thatching and rick-thatching are two very different jobs, although in principle there is often some relation between them.

AN OLD THATCHER AT WORK.

In repairing old thatch the fresh straw or reeds are simply pegged and tied with spicks and twine into the old thatch; but when a new house or cottage is to be thatched, layers of straw (often called the inner coat or waistcoat), to which the final thatch is fastened, have first to be sewn on to the rafters to a thickness of at least a foot.

Two men are always required, one inside and one outside the rafters, using tar-rope and a steel needle a foot or more in length for this work. The man inside gives a tap to show where his hand is, and the man outside puts through the needle cautiously, lest he should injure the other. The rope is in this way wound round and round the horizontal rafters firmly sewing on the inner coat. With this finished, the roof is then thatched in a similar way to a rick. As each layer of straw is laid on it is raked down with the thatching-comb and the butts are brought level with the leggett or biddle and finished off with the paring-knife.

The final layer of straw or reed is laid very carefully, especially round the corners, or over dormers, where it is given a slight twist so that the rain may shoot off the ends of the straw and not settle into the hollows. This thatch is fixed with spicks driven into the " waistcoat " in much the same manner as in rick thatching, care being taken to see that they are inclined upwards a little so as not to make holes for the rain to get in. The thatch is finally held down by slats of split hazel fixed by single-twist spicks. These are often laid in a diamond formation, the operation being known as " dementing."

In some districts the method of " herring-boning " in place of " dementing " is used to make other fancy patterns; and the working of the edges of the outer layers of thatch into ornamental shapes has also been introduced by many highly skilled members of the craft.

Straw and reed must have provided one of the very earliest roofs for human habitations; but by a strange turn of the wheel of fortune only the rich can afford to thatch their homes to-day and shelter under a roof which, not many years ago, was considered good enough only for the very humble.

For centuries the thatcher's art has contributed a great part of the charm to our English villages, and although there are now many other materials used for roofing, there

SOME ANCIENT COUNTRY CRAFTS

THATCH LIKE WAVES OF A ROLLING SEA, HEREFORDSHIRE.

are still some thousands of these picturesque old thatched roofs to be seen.

In house-thatching there is, of course, an endless variety of designs favoured by individual craftsmen; "halfmoons," "buckles," "sawteeth," "scallops" and "moons" are a few of the names given to the different patterns. It is, in fact, rare to find, even in the same village, two thatched roofs exactly alike.

Some old roofs come down very low, in a long sweep from the ridge-pole, and the little windows peep forth shyly from beneath luxuriant tresses of straw or reed. There are heavy, solid roofs of thatch that cover a cottage as an extinguisher covers a candle; there are others broken up by well-shaped "eyebrows" over the upper windows or by separate little gables of thatch that shelter the projecting dormers. That is the very essence of their charm—their infinite variety, their unfailing originality.

It is of little avail for anyone to tell us that thatched roofs are not healthy, that they breed too many insects, that they are too easily fired by a chance spark, etc. etc. There is a peculiar charm about an old thatched roof which renders all arguments unavailing, even if they are justified. For here is a matter in which sentiment and feeling take the upper hand of cold reason.

Chapter XI

COUNTRY CURIOS

Old cottages and farmhouses are, besides being interesting in themselves, real treasure houses for seekers after rural "bygones." Such items as love spoons, fire-backs, horse brasses and lace bobbins are occasionally to be secured for a mere song and make a most interesting collection.

The term "spooning" is familiar enough, but how many people know its origin? The objects shown in the illustration supply the explanation. They are carved wood betrothal spoons, and are to be found in many parts of Great Britain. These spoons were made by rustic swains and presented to their "intendeds" as a proposal of marriage.

Old iron fire-backs are another interesting item often seen in the large fireplaces of some cottages. Fire-backs were made in great numbers during the fifteenth and sixteenth centuries, principally in Sussex, when the iron industry flourished in that county.

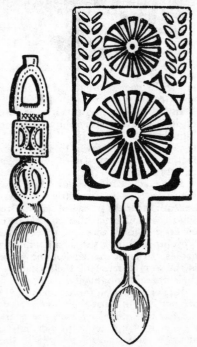

LOVE-SPOONS.
Welsh Type. Early English, 18th cent.

Many excellent specimens also hail from the **Forest of Dean**, where iron was also worked.

The designs on the fire-backs are often crude and meaningless, but sometimes they are very effective, and nearly always interesting. The stock ornaments of the moulders were fleur-de-lys, rosettes, daggers, shields, crowns, etc., while short lengths of twisted cable are a common characteristic of many fire-backs.

Various methods were employed in making the moulds from which the backs were cast. The most primitive was to make an impression in sand with a board cut to the required outline and thickness. The molten iron was then poured into the shallow cavity, without any top mould, in much the same way as a sow of iron is made at the present time.

Some of the fire-backs made during the second half of the sixteenth century were of much improved design, as the one in the illustration shows. This specimen, cast in relief, is decorated with the Royal Arms and Supporters of Queen Elizabeth. (It will be noted that one of the supporters is a dragon ; this was later changed to the unicorn.) It is inscribed, " Made in Sussex by John Harvo," and stands three feet six inches in height.

THE CROOK

The shepherd's crook, that indispensable trademark of his craft, is another item of peculiar interest to the wayfarer which can occasionally be examined when visiting some old cottage or barn.

There is less variety among the shapes of modern sheep-crooks than among ancient types. A number of blacksmiths, however, still make them and some have their own designs.

TWO SPECIMENS OF CROOKS.

The earliest known crooks were fashioned entirely of wood and were probably first introduced into England by the Crusaders when they returned from the East. Old British crooks were made of wrought iron, with a staff of ash some five or six feet in length. Brass crooks once came on the market, but their popularity was shortlived, for a shepherd expects one crook to last his lifetime or even longer.

SUSSEX IRON FIRE-BACK, 16th CENT.

One of the best known types of crooks was made by a smith named Berry, during the early nineteenth century, at a little forge in the village of Pyecombe, in Sussex. These Pyecombe Crooks are famous among shepherds all the world over.

Many of these crooks are now museum pieces and highly prized, but one may still occasionally discover, hidden away in some corner of a cottage or barn, a long forgotten specimen. Berry was a very fine craftsman and his crooks fifty years ago were as necessary to the Southdown shepherd in life as was the tuft of sheep's wool which was buried with him as an explanation of his absence from church on Sundays.

COUNTRY CURIOS

THE WILTSHIRE SHEEP BELL.

SHEEP BELLS

Old Sheep Bells made by the village blacksmith are another curiosity worth hunting for. Sheep Bells can still be heard in many counties, where the difficulty of locating the flocks among the hills and hollows makes them indeed a necessity ; but most of them are now factory products.

The old bells illustrated here are items from my own collection of rural "bygones." I found the first in a village shop in Wiltshire. This type of bell was, I believe, also used in Buckinghamshire and other counties. It is the product of some village smithy and has been fashioned from sheet iron, which has been bent to shape and the end of the material welded together ; the join can clearly be seen down the middle of one side of the bell. As may be imagined, a bell wrought in this fashion does not produce a very musical note ; but it was quite effective for the purpose for which it was intended. The tongue is a roughly-shaped "blob" of metal hung from a hook riveted to the top of the bell.

The other specimen was discovered in Sussex and is also made of sheet iron ; but in this case the edges of the folded metal are only riveted together at the sides of the bell. The handle is simply a loop of metal on to the inside part of which the roughly made tongue is hooked.

THE SUSSEX SHEEP BELL.

Both these bells were made, I suppose, not later than the eighteenth century, for by the nineteenth century small bells could be bought so cheaply from the factories that it would not have been worth while to have one specially made by the local blacksmith.

It is strange how hard tradition clings ! This old sheep bell I discovered in Wiltshire, made for a commonplace

THE WILLOW PATTERN WARE.

agricultural purpose, is identical in general shape with some of the oldest bells in existence. It is of a type far more ancient—in Britain, if not in other countries—than the round type with the splayed-out lip which has for so long been in vogue for church bells and for most other kinds of bells. The Wiltshire bell is rectangular instead of circular in plan, with two broad sides and two narrow ones. You also find the same shape in some Irish bells known to date back at least as far as the ninth century. Even the shape of the handle is the same as those of bells used more than a thousand years ago.

WILLOW PATTERN WARE

Another interesting curio often to be found among the treasures of some old-world cottage or farmhouse is a piece of genuine Willow Pattern Ware. Many people have the idea that this ware is of Chinese origin ; but although the design certainly has a Chinese atmosphere about it, it was, nevertheless, created by an Englishman named Thomas Turner. He first produced it about 1780 at his pottery works in Caughley, near Bridgnorth, Shropshire, and, if rumour be correct, the first pieces were specially made to the order of a wealthy gentleman named Whitmore.

The design is in blue on a white or bluish-white ground and was called by Turner the Nankin design. It soon became very fashionable in England. Later the name was changed to the Willow Pattern and by some means or other a quaint story came into being concerning the scene depicted. This story is of a mandarin's daughter, and runs as follows :

There was once a beautiful Chinese girl named Koong Shee, whose father, a wealthy mandarin, wished her to marry another rich merchant of his choice, whom Koong Shee greatly disliked. The maiden had already fallen deeply in love with her father's secretary, a young man who was both handsome and brave, but who was unfortunately very poor. His name was Chang.

Koong Shee's father, being determined that she should do as he wished, locked her up, in disgrace, in a little summer house at the end of his large garden. Languishing sadly, Koong Shee watched the blossom of the apple tree slowly fade and grow into apples and had almost given up all hope of marrying her lover ; but Chang was a resourceful young man, and although he could not get to her or talk with her he managed to send a love letter beseeching her to fly with him. Koong Shee received the letter and answered it with another, which said that if Chang was brave enough and really loved her, he would come to her aid.

That evening, Chang rescued his love from her dainty prison ; but just as they were escaping over the bridge— the girl with her distaff and the lover carrying her jewel box

—the angry father saw them and gave chase, armed with a whip.

This is the scene on the Willow Pattern china. The lovers are crossing the little bridge, with the infuriated father close on their heels. You can see the rich and disappointed merchant coming rapidly to the rescue in a boat.

Well, the story says that Koong Shee and Chang escaped and lived very happily in a little house across the lake. But one night, the rich suitor, in his rage, set fire to the little house with Koong Shee and Chang inside. The gods, however, took pity on the lovers and turned them into two doves, which flew away to enjoy immortal bliss in Heaven.

TOBY JUGS

A Toby Jug is another interesting piece of old china well worth adding to your collection. Tradition has it that this grotesque piece of Staffordshire ware was named after a notorious eighteenth-century drinker, Henry Elwes, nick-named Toby Fillpot on account of his drinking capacities.

A TYPICAL TOBY JUG.

The original Toby jug, which first made its appearance about 1749, was used for holding beer and was in the form of a stout figure of a man wearing a cocked hat and knee-breeches, and generally embodied a variety of glazed colourings. A typical example shows a squat little figure attired in a purple coat, green waistcoat, yellow breeches and white stockings. There are also about two dozen variations in the design of the figures known to the collectors of Toby Jugs which have recognised values according to their artistic merits and their rarity.

In addition to the Toby Fillpot, there are jugs modelled in the likeness of a Watchman in a long grey coat and black hat, with his lantern in hand, a Sailor dressed in blue, seated on a chest of gold, a Postboy astride a barrel, the Squire seated with pipe and jug, the Hearty Good Fellow in yellow breeches, blue coat and striped waistcoat, the Convict, a very thin man in yellow stripes, and the One Armed Toby. Then there is Toby's wife, Joan, in brown bodice, yellow apron, and tall mobcap, regarded as a great prize among collectors, for female Tobies are very rare. Dwarf Tobies, less than four inches in height, were also made.

Occasionally, inscriptions can be found on the small jug held in Toby's left hand. ' Drink your ale up, cock your tail up,' was very popular, while the word " Stingo," a type of strong ale, was sometimes inscribed on the jug.

In addition to jugs, there are Toby mugs, inkpots, salt-cellars, mustard pots and teapots, all modelled in the likeness of that rotund, burlesque, antique personage, old Toby Fillpot.

PILLOW LACE AND BOBBINS

Pillow-lace bobbins are an interesting item occasionally discovered among the treasures in some old cottage. These quaint little objects—as commonplace and untreasured a couple of generations ago as tea-caddies and candle-snuffers, and such like everyday household trifles—have now attained the rather pathetic dignity of inclusion among the stocks of antique dealers, and are even finding their place in some of our museums.

I possess a small collection among my rural " bygones," and have found much pleasure in my endeavours to ascertain from which part of the country they originated ; for if you study the subject you will discover that distinct types of bobbins are favoured by pillow-lace makers in different parts of the country. In Huntingdonshire, for instance, the bobbins were almost always made of bone, the lower end usually taking the form of a little turned knob, through which a hole was bored and a piece of wire threaded on which one strung glass beads, coins and other small oddments. The attachments are called " jingles " or " spangles " and are always to be found on the Huntingdonshire bobbins. Devonshire lace bobbins, on the other hand, are, I believe, usually made of wood, decorated with shallow, incised rings and with stained patterns. They do not, so far as my knowledge goes, have jingles. In Oxfordshire the bobbins frequently have " jingles." In that county they are them-selves made of wood, but are of quite a different pattern from those of Devonshire.

On some of the bobbins, more especially those of Hunting-donshire, are inscribed dates, and sometimes names, thus forming interesting mementoes of events and persons in the families in which they were used. Among the specimens from my own small collection illustrated here,

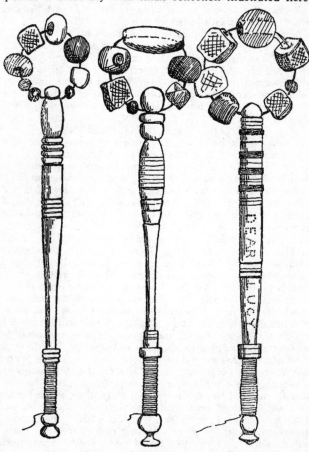

PILLOW-LACE BOBBINS.

one is inscribed " Dear Lucy," and probably dates from about the middle of the nineteenth century.

The process by which the lace is made on the pillow is roughly as follows. A pattern is first drawn upon a piece of paper or parchment, which is afterwards attached to the pillow. Pins are then stuck in at regular intervals in the lines of the pattern and the threads of the bobbins are twisted or plaited round them so as to form the network arrangement which is so characteristic of this type of lace.

There are very many exquisite and intricate designs made in pillow-lace, but as this little volume is merely a scrapbook, and not an encyclopædia, it is useless to attempt a full description of them here. If however, during your wandering in some out-of-the-way village, you have the good fortune to come across some old lady who still possesses the art of pillow-lace making, it will well repay you to spend an hour or so in her company and watch her at work.

HORSE BRASSES

Those of you who have visited an agricultural show or the cart horse parade in Regent's Park, London, on Whit Monday, must have admired the wonderful variety of decorative brass discs that adorn the harness of the magnificent animals.

These discs are usually called sun-brasses or metals by the carters, but occasionally you hear them spoken of as amulets, a word which gives a slight clue to their supposed origin. At one time their purpose was to act as charms to keep away the evil eye and all other undesirable occult influences. Nowadays they are looked upon purely as ornamental and, incidentally, interesting articles to collect ; or is it just possible that some old teamster would regard the loss of one of his brasses as prophetic of some ill luck in store for him or for his horses ?

Most antiquarians agree that their origin is extremely ancient, some supposing them to be referred to in the Bible (Judges VIII, 21-26), which is said to have been written 1450 B.C. It is known that they were used in Roman times in Europe and the Near East, when their magical purpose was considered to be of great importance and their decorative effect quite secondary. Their history since those times is practically continuous and to-day they are found in one form or another in many corners of the world.

In our own country, as already mentioned, they are to be seen mostly on the harness of the farm and heavy draught horses. As many as forty of these brasses may be worn by any horse in full dress, but a more ordinary set consists of

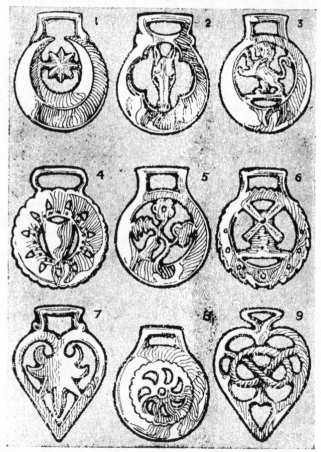

HORSE BRASSES.

two ear brasses, from five to ten on the mortingale or breast strap, three suspended from straps on each shoulder and occasionally one on the forehead.   A special form, known as a " terret " or " flyer," is occasionally worn on top of the horse's head and is considered to be a conventionalised remnant of the stately plumes worn by all the war-horses of the Middle Ages.

It is in the designs used in many of the brasses that the early magical significance is most apparent.   Many hundred odd varieties which are estimated to exist trace back to the sun's disc, to the crescent moon or to the conventional heart, each of which is a symbol of magical influence according to folklore.   Sometimes stars of seven, eight or ten rays are used and occasionally purely geometrical figures.   Designs incorporating birds and animals are quite common, the horse naturally taking the lead, cats, dogs, deer, swans, eagles and even bee-hives are found.

Flowers appear but rarely, the commonest being the combined Rose, Thistle and Shamrock.   Heraldic designs are occasionally seen on the harness of horses on large private estates and also as local survivals of historic families which may now have been lost sight of.

Some of the ornaments more or less tell their own story, as in the case of the " occupational " brasses, where the mill and the shepherd with his crook often denote that the horse wearing these decorations belonged to a miller and a farmer respectively.

Women rarely appear in these designs, but in the discs, often referred to as commemorative brasses, portraits of Queen Victoria are to be found, together with those of kings and other famous people.

And now for a few details that will help any of you who want to begin collecting, but know little about your subject.

In the first place, brasses can be divided into two distinct classes, the old ones which were cast in moulds, and the new ones which are stamped out by machinery.   The latter are of much less interest than the former and are at present hardly worth bothering with.

The old ones can usually be identified by the stubs on the back which are the points at which the molten metal was poured into the mould ; in addition to this they are generally smooth on the front only, the back being roughened and pock-marked from the moulding process.

ELF-DARTS

The accompanying little illustration is of a small object given to me, to add to my collection of country curios, by an old lady living in Ireland. It consists of a small flint arrow-head—one inch long by half an inch wide—with barbs removed, and mounted in a silver fitting with ring attached.

In many parts of the world, stone implements, found by metal-using savages, or by uneducated folk of civilised countries, were often regarded as objects of mysterious origin possessed of magical properties and were carried or worn as amulets or charms against poison and witchcraft.

In many out-of-the-way places in Great Britain, these arrow-head charms are still known to the country folk as elf-bolts or elf-darts, the belief being at one time that they were shot by malicious elves or fairies, at men and cattle.

Both in Scotland and Ireland, cattle were believed to fall sick through being struck by one of these elf-darts, and a quack doctor, having felt the animal all over, would usually produce one of these flints from its skin as proof of the cure. Boiling one or more arrow-heads in water, and administering this to the cattle was another method by which a cure was often effected by these quack doctors.

ELF-DART.

Stone celts were also looked upon in many parts as " thunder-bolts " and were much prized as charms with the power of protecting the owner's house and property against lightning-strokes.

It was not until the early part of the eighteenth century that, even among the educated in Europe, prehistoric stone implements began to be recognised for what they are ; and it was not until about the middle of the following century that progress began to be made in unearthing and interpreting the evidence that we now possess concerning these ancient weapons.

CHAPTER XII

FACTS, FANCY AND FALLACY

SUPERSTITIONS

Alas ! you know the cause too well ;
The salt is spilt, to me it fell.
Then to contribute to my loss,
My knife and fork were laid across ;
On Friday, too ! the day I dread ;
Would I were safe at home, in bed !
Last night (I vow to heaven 'tis true)
Bounce from the fire a coffin flew.
Next post some fatal news shall tell :
God send my Cornish friends be well !

GAY.

In many villages and outlying districts the older inhabitants
are firm believers in all sorts of odd superstitions and quaint
old customs.

Our ancestors always regarded the bee as possessing
almost supernatural powers, and their reverence for these
valuable insects doubtless originated the surprising number
of superstitions connected with them. One of these, of
which many of you may have heard, is the very ancient
custom of " Telling the Bees " of a death in the family ·

" Bees ! Bees ! Hark to your bees !
  Hide from your neighbours as much as you please,
  But all that has happened, to us you must tell,
  Or else we will give you no honey to sell ! "

KIPLING.

In some villages it is believed that unless the creatures
have this news " announced " to them properly they will
all die or desert the hive. I once heard this done. An old

lady of seventy-eight went solemnly round her bee-hives, tapped the top of each skep and said in very solemn tones, "Queen Bee! Queen Bee! Queen Bee! William's wife, my daughter-in-law, is dead." A little crepe bow is occasionally fastened on the hive so as to put the bees properly into mourning when the head of a family dies, and many curious stories are told of bad fortune following neglect of these precautions. In some parts of Yorkshire, the bees are actually invited to attend their master's funeral, and in some neighbourhoods the insects have to be told personally by the heir for whom they must work in future.

When bees swarm or leave their hive unexpectedly, it is often believed that something has offended them. For this reason they are treated always as members of the household and are often told all-important family news.

Suffolk's superstition concerning bees is that it is unlucky for a swarm to settle on anyone's premises if they are not later claimed by the real owner. In Rutlandshire, England's smallest county, it is regarded as a sure sign of a stranger coming to the house if a bumble bee flies in at the window; and in Lancashire to dream of bees means good luck.

TELLING THE BEES.

FACTS, FANCY AND FALLACY

These and many other quaint superstitions concerning the bees are firmly believed in by the older country folk, who say that, the bees are never wrong !

" Never burn green ! " is another saying of the old country-women when they see the younger folk burning up wilted flowers or cabbage stalks. These old people will bury their green refuse but not risk the doom which attends burning it. It is, however, unlucky to leave up Christmas decorations of holly and evergreen after Twelfth Night, and this greenery may be safely burnt.

Turning to the plant world, of all trees the elder has the worst repute, as the tree on which Judas hanged himself, and is hence accursed. Yet you earn three years bad luck if you cut it down. There is also an old country tradition that lightning will not strike an elder tree, because this was the tree from which the Cross of Christ was made. It is for this reason that some country folk will not use elder sticks to kindle a fire and will not carry them inside their houses.

Again, it is most unlucky to bring hawthorn indoors. Yet another superstition is that good luck is due to the person who receives a gift of may blossom on May Day ; but the season has to be very forward for this flower to be picked so early in the year. In the old days a hedger would never cut oak, ash or holly, and many people can recall when hedges contained numerous saplings of these trees. Oak, ash and holly are traditionally sacred. " When the gorse is out of flower, kissing's out of favour." But who has ever known the countryside lacking a single gorse bloom ? Nobody has !

Shepherds never count their lambs till after tailing and castrating are finished. Numbering the lambs is felt to court calamity. Should a stranger count the lambs the shepherd will cross the fingers of his left hand to frustrate the evil spirits which, by counting, have got power over his flock. But there is, I think, more in this superstition than meets the eye, for the other day a shepherd acquaintance lifted the veil. He confessed he did not count his lambs because it brought bad luck. " But there's more to it than that, master. If I count my lambs and I tell the boss how many there are from day to day and I get some bad luck, where am I ? But if the boss don't know how many lambs are born, how's he going to know how many die, eh ? "

147

BIRD SUPERSTITIONS AND OMENS

THE CROMER ARMS.

There are many quaint superstitions and omens connected with birds that are, even in these unromantic days, still firmly believed in by many country folk. All down the ages, members of the crow family have been infamous as birds of ill-omen, a reputation which is no doubt mainly due to their colour and carrion habits.

In ancient mythology the raven stands out pre-eminently among all other members of this family as being a foreboder of misfortune. According to Greek legend the raven was not always black. It was once white and had the colour of its plumage changed by one of the gods as a punishment for tittle-tattling. In the very early days a raven is supposed to have told the god Apollo that Coronis, a Thessalian nymph whom he dearly loved, had been unfaithful to him. Apollo, on hearing this, flew into a rage, and searching out the inconstant nymph, slew her with a dart. But hating the tell-tale bird:

" He blacked the raven o'er
And bid him prate in his white plumes no more."

In olden times ravens were also supposed to possess the gift of being able to foretell approaching death. Cicero was forewarned of his impending death by the fluttering of a raven over him. Macaulay relates the legend that a raven entered the chamber of the great orator on the day of his murder, and pulled the clothes off his bed.

In more recent times, Marlowe tells how—

" The sad presaging raven tolls
The sick man's passport in her beak
And in the shadow of the silent night
Doth shake contagion from her sable wings."

Shakespeare also has reference to the raven when he makes Lady Macbeth say:

FACTS, FANCY AND FALLACY

" The raven himself is hoarse that croaks the fatal **entrance**
of Duncan under my battlements."

In common with other members of the corvidæ **family**,
these birds were thought to be able to divine hands **stained**
with human blood.   Macbeth is made to say in the **Ghost**
scene to Lady Macbeth :

" Augurs, and understood relations, have
    By magot-pies, and choughs and rooks brought forth
    The secret'st man of blood."

Among some of the older folk of Buckinghamshire it **is**
still considered unlucky to see one magpie, but lucky **to see**
two ; while in certain districts on the borders of **England**
and Wales, and in Yorkshire, one occasionally hears **this**
rhyme about magpies :

" One for sorrow, two for mirth,
    Three for a wedding and four for a birth,
    Five for silver, six for gold,
    Seven for a secret ne'er to be told."

Another version of the same rhyme finishes up :

" Five poverty, six wealth,
    Seven the very devil himself."

As an instance
of superstitions
about the crow,
it may be cited
that a year or so
ago the fishermen
of Cromer pro-
tested that the
image of the
crow which the
council had erec-
ted as the wind
direction-finder
of a weather vane
was a bird of

The Raven (A Bird of Ill-omen).

ill-omen and that as soon as it was put up their catches of crabs and lobsters had fallen off. Landsmen, too, urged the council to remove the vane, saying that the crow was a symbol of " Death, disaster and destruction " ; and notwithstanding the fact that the town's coat-of-arms bears three crows as charges, the " Evil Crow " on the weather vane was removed, much to the relief of many of the inhabitants.

The crow, from Roman times at least, has been a bird of ill-omen. Its croaking was held to foretell rain and bad weather—a Nature observation mentioned by Virgil, the great Roman epic poet who died in 19 B.C., in one of the books of the Georgics. In flight or in alighting the crow might be a portent of almost any disaster.

The comparative rarity of the solitary crow, hooded or carrion, in England, has probably preserved for them this sinister reputation, which the sociable rook has avoided, and local rhymes tell of the conclusions to be drawn from their flight. Thus, in Essex the following jingle occurs :

> " One's unlucky,
> Two's lucky,
> Three is health,
> Four is wealth,
> Five is sickness,
> And six is death."

In many parts of Europe, the superstition that crows are connected with bad luck is met with. One crow cawing on the roof of the house where a sick person lies is held to foreshadow his death. In parts of Switzerland, the perching of a crow on the house in which there is a corpse is thought to show that the soul of the dead is irrevocably damned.

In another ancient literary work, Hesiod (" Works and Days," 746-747), the hatred of the crow is referred to in a rather obscure passage. " Do not when building a house leave it unplaned lest the noisy crow come and caw thereon." It is not quite clear what " unplaned " signifies ; but that the crow was unwelcome is obvious.

In Kent there is a belief that if a house martin enters a house all the inhabitants will be fortunate thereafter. The robin's cry, in a sad note, is equally supposed to indicate sickness and possibly death.

RED SKY AT NIGHT IS THE SHEPHERD'S DELIGHT.

The robin is very well known to ornithologists to be a pugnacious little bird. It is, indeed, said that he will attack the eyes of any intruder who may venture to molest his nest.

Similarly, the common wren has been held by country folk to possess supernatural powers. If a finger touches the eggs in a wren's nest, local belief avers that that finger will wither and die.

In my childhood, while blue tits were welcomed as harbingers of happiness, the owl screeching near a house was supposed to presage disaster.

WEATHER LORE

If Ducks and Drakes their Wings do flutter high,
Or tender Colts upon their Backs do lye ;
If Sheep do bleat, or play, or skip about,
Or Swine hide Straw by bearing on their Snout ;
If Oxen lick themselves against the Hair,
Or grazing Kine to feed apace appear,
If Cattle bellow, gazing from below,
Or if Dog's Entrails rumble to and fro ;
If Doves or Pigeons in the Evening come
Later than usual to their Dove house home ;
If Crows and Daws do oft themselves be-wet
Or Ants and   ismires home apace do go ;
If in the Dust Hens do their Pinions shake,

Or by their flocking a great Number make ;
If Swallows fly upon the Water low,
Or Wood-Lice seem in Armies for to go ;
If Flies, or Gnats, or Fleas infest and bite,
Or sting more than they're wont by Day and Night ;
If Toads hie home, or Frogs do croak amain,
Or Peacocks cry : Soon after look for Rain.
" The New Book of Knowledge, 1758."

In these enlightened days, when wireless plays such an important part in our lives, many of us have fallen into the habit of relying on the official weather report, with the result that we have ceased to make our own observations of wind and cloud, and other natural signs, to obtain our forecast. But in the days when wireless was unknown, everyone, especially country folk, had to rely entirely on personal observation to foretell the weather.

One of the results of this old habit is that many quaint rhymes and jingles have come into being concerning the weather. In fact, a vast volume could be filled if all the weather sayings of the nations were gathered together, and many are dependent on open-air observations of the sky and of nature.

Probably the best known saying is the following (sometimes with slight variations) :

" Red sky in the morning is the shepherd's warning ;
Red sky at night is the shepherd's delight."

One of the oldest examples of weather lore is to be found in the New Testament (Matthew XVI, 2, 3) :

" When it is evening ye say, It will be fair weather, for the sky is red. And in the morning, It will be foul weather to-day, for the sky is red and lowering."

So much for the antiquity of this piece of weather lore ; but the idea is just as widespread as it is ancient, for it is found as an English saying, as a Scotch couplet, in French, German and Italian. A common variation of the wording is :

" Evening red and morning grey
Will set the traveller on his way.
Evening grey and morning red
Brings down rain upon his head."

FACTS, FANCY AND FALLACY

A wet morning is, however, not always the forerunner of a wet day ; there is often truth (subject to other indications) in the saying :

"Rain before seven, fine before eleven."

From the enormous number of weather proverbs it is necessary to pick out those that contain evidence of keen observation backed by just reasoning.

The variations of the following quotation are legion, as in every locality the name of the nearest hilltop is used :

"When Lookout Mountain has its cap on, it will rain in six hours."

Sailors, as might be expected, have many rhymes concerning the weather, especially with regard to the wind :

"When the rain's before the wind
Topsail halliards you must mind.
When the wind's before the rain
Then all standing may remain."

The familiar saying :

"Keep buttoned to chin till May be in. Ne'er cast a clout till May be out."

has often raised the query as to what is meant by "May." Is it the blossom or the month ? One explanation is that the word "May" in the first line refers to the month, and in the second line to the blossom. This seems to be reasonable, as the blossom is rarely out until the month is well advanced.

NE'ER CAST A CLOUT . . .

CHAPTER XIII

QUAINT COUNTRY CUSTOMS

OAK APPLE DAY

THE old customs that May brings with it are both varied and interesting. There is one, however, which has, I fear, shown signs of decline in recent years. I refer to the observance of Oak Apple Day. This custom was instituted in memory of King Charles II's picturesque escape from pursuing Roundheads, after the battle of Worcester, by hiding in the branches of an oak tree at Boscobel, on the borders of Staffordshire. It was not until nine years later that Oak Apple Day was first celebrated, on May 29th, 1660, King Charles's thirtieth birthday and the day on which he was restored to the throne of England.

Some thirty years ago, " Show your oak ! " was the cry heard in country places on that morning in May ; and it was necessary to sport a sprig of oak in one's cap or buttonhole in fulfilment of a then firmly established custom.

Even in these modern times, however, there is one place that never forgets King Charles II. That place is the Royal Hospital for Army Pensioners at Chelsea, founded by King Charles himself. Here the King's effigy is symbolically concealed in a mass of oak branches, while the Pensioners march past it at the salute, each wearing a sprig of oak, and are rewarded for their loyalty to their benefactor by receiving double rations at dinner.

Although Oak Apple Day is gradually slipping out of recognition, like so many other quaint old customs, we have at least scores of " Royal Oak " inns all over the country to preserve by their name the memory of the Boscobel incident of 1651. The name Boscobel has its origin in the Italian words " *bosco bello*," (beautiful wood).

" GROVELY, GROVELY, AND ALL GROVELY "

Another quaint old Oak Apple Day custom, which fortunately still survives, is observed in the little village of Wishford, and the adjoining village of Barford, a few miles from Salisbury, in Wiltshire. It dates from very ancient days and used, at one time, to be held at Whitsun ; but it now takes place on May 29th. The story of its origin is very interesting.

Centuries ago, the people of these little villages had the right to gather as much wood as they could carry from the nearby Grovely Woods. At one period Grovely came under

THE BOSCOBEL OAK.

the ownership of the Earls of Pembroke, who objected to this old custom. But for many years nothing definite was done to stop it, until finally, one Earl, bolder than his ancestors, gave orders that no more wood was to be gathered. The villagers were much perturbed, but no man dared to disobey the order of the lordly gentleman. Not so a woman ! Grace Reed, a well known character of the village, openly defied the Earl and, with two or three companions, went as usual to the woods and gathered her fuel. A few days later, a summons was served on her. She, however, refused to pay the fine, and was put into prison.

Then the unexpected happened. The very next day she was set free, with no other explanation beyond the fact that a mistake had been made. The Earl had evidently been informed by some higher authority that he had no power to forbid the right of the people.

From that day the villagers have always celebrated the event, and on Oak Apple Day they uphold their right of gathering wood for the coming year by carrying out the following quaint custom.

At sunrise, men, women and children proceed, in a body, to Grovely Woods, and cut down boughs of oak, which they carry or drag back along the rough road to the village. These they set up outside their cottages for good luck, and so wholeheartedly do they enjoy the ceremony that you will not find one door lintel without its lucky mascot. In no time the village has put on quite a festive appearance with flags and bunting. And then, at midday, another procession is formed. Some of the elders of the village lead the way, bearing a banner inscribed with the words " GROVELY, GROVELY, AND ALL GROVELY." Next come four women, bearing on their heads bundles of firewood. Then follows a large company of men, each carrying a huge bough of oak on his shoulders, till the road looks like a moving forest. They, in turn, are followed by the Maypole dancers and other members of the community.

Around the picturesque little village, with its beautiful old thatched cottages, they wend their way, past the stately thirteenth century church, and on to a large field where the maypole stands. Here follows all the usual fun of the fair, with maypole dancing and other attractions. And so, once again, as the sun sets on the festivities, the villagers of

Wishford have preserved their right to gather " dry, snappy sticks " from Grovely for another year.

THE DANCE OF THE DEERMEN

The Horn Dance, or Dance of the Deermen, which is performed at Abbots Bromley, in Staffordshire, is another pleasing custom which also seems to have some connection with the preservation of the rights of the people. The exact origin is somewhat obscure. It may once have been part of a totemic ritual of our hunting ancestors ; but the theory which is more generally accepted is that it arose from the determination of the people of Abbots Bromley to prove that they had the right to hunt deer in the surrounding Needwood Forest. For it must be remembered that at one time deer played an important part in our national life, and the loss of the right to hunt them would have been a serious matter to the inhabitants. The fact that the horns which

DEERMAN DANCE. A SET OF ANTLERS.

are carried by some of the dancers are reindeer antlers, seems to date the custom back at least to Saxon times, for reindeer have been extinct in this country for quite a thousand years.

The performers are twelve in number, all males. Six are deermen, and carry the antlers set in wooden heads and mounted on short poles. Their costume is a cutaway jerkin, Tudor cap, and knickers, patterned with oak leaves and acorns, a decoration which seems to confirm the connection with the forest.

The other performers are as follows   A lad mounted on

a hobby-horse; a youthful archer with wooden bow and arrow who represents Robin Hood, and, naturally, Maid Marian. "She" has a white, skirted costume, below which show the turn-ups of grey flannel trousers. The "maid" has the important task of collecting the money from the onlookers and does not take any active part in the dance. A fool in cap and bells, a musician with concertina, and another with a triangle, complete the cast.

The inclusion of Robin Hood and Maid Marian would date the dance from Richard I's reign; but Dr. Plot, who mentions the dance in his "Natural History of Staffordshire," 1686, makes no reference to Robin Hood and Maid Marian, nor to the musicians, but indicates that the man on the hobby-horse wielded the bow and arrow, which rather suggests that these characters are a subsequent introduction.

The music of the Horn Dance is one of the most haunting of our traditional tunes. It has a chanting sound and is aided by the twanging of the arrow on the bow and the slapping of the horse's head with a whip.

At one time the dance was celebrated on Christmas Day, New Year's Day and Twelfth Day; but it is now performed on the Monday after Wakes Sunday, the Sunday following September 4th.

The performers gather at the "Goat's Head," a fine, half-timbered inn in the market square of Abbots Bromley, and make a tour of the surrounding countryside, going the round of farms and houses and performing the dance at each. Towards evening they return to the market square where, after an interval for refreshments at the "Goat's Head," the final performance takes place.

The dance is quite a simple affair; following in single file behind the leading deerman, the dancers make a circular movement, from which they break into two lines, facing one another a few yards apart. The lines advance and retire several times, while the archer pretends to shoot the deer; a further circling movement, and the dancers move a little further along the road, where the dance is repeated.

All the properties—the horns, the hobby-horse, and bow and arrow—connected with the dance, belong to the Vicar of the Parish during his incumbency, and are kept in the church tower when not in use.

PLOUGH BOY

Plough Monday, next after that Twelfthtide is past,
Bids out with the plough, the worst husband is last ;
If ploughman gets hatchet or whip to the screen,
Maids loseth their cock if no water be seen.*

Agricultural labourers were at one time expected to return to their avocations after the festivities of Christmas on Plough Monday, i.e. the first Monday after Old Christmas Day (January 6th),† and in this connection another old custom was observed.

Groups of farm labourers, after adorning themselves with ribbons and blackening their faces, used to parade the village at dusk, dragging a decorated plough from door to door as they chanted their weird incantation, to an accompaniment on tin trays, etc., in the hope of collecting " plough money," to be spent in a frolic.

> Tinka-boy, plough-boy,
> Only once a year !
> Gi's tuppence-ha'penny to buy a pint of beer !
> If not tuppence-ha'penny a penny will do !
> If not a penny still God bless you.

Another variation with the same idea runs as follows :

" Have ye got a penny for a poor old plough boy, plough
boy ?
If ye haven't got a penny, a ha'penny will do,
If ye haven't got a ha'penny then God bless you
We'll tear your threshold up and plough your doorway
through and through ! "

But the villagers only smiled at one another reassuringly, knowing that yet again the yearly threat would remain unexecuted.

Unfortunately the practice is not so generally observed these days ; but in one or two out-of-the-way villages it is still carried on by the younger members of the community,

---

* If the ploughman on Plough Monday could get any of his implements to the fireside before the maid put on her kettle, she forfeited her shrovetide cock.

† January 6th, Epiphany. The day on which the infant Jesus met the Three Wise Men.

although they no longer carry the plough with which to plough up the doorsteps of those who refuse to give.

One quaint rhyme I heard only a year or so ago, in Buckinghamshire, in connection with Plough Monday, runs as follows :

"O, O, E, I, O,
Up with the shovel and the hoe,
Down with the fiddle and the drum.
No more work for poor old neddy,
Now that the ploughing's done."

THE WAYFARER'S DOLE

There are very few survivals of the past with so quaint and interesting a history as the distribution of the " Wayfarer's Dole," which takes place every day at the picturesque Hospice of the Brethren of St. Cross, near Winchester, Hampshire.

The dole was founded in 1136 by the Bishop of Winchester, Henry de Blois, the grandson of William the Conqueror, who built the hospice for the maintenance of " 13 poor men, unable to work, who have followed humble but honest pursuits, that they may be cared for and provided with garments and beds suitable to their infirmities."

The hospice was also to give food and drink daily to one hundred poor wanderers who came to its gates, with the result that for the past seven hundred years or more any tired and weary wayfarer has had the right to knock on the ancient oak door and to be served by one of the Brethren with a horn of good old English home-brewed ale and a portion of bread.   Any wayfarer may witness the ceremony of giving away the dole, which is dispensed at the Porter's lodge, under the ancient Norman archway, and as it is given without any questions being asked, the " weary " rambler is not excluded from being served.

Hidden away as it is, the hospice is easily passed by those hurrying along the main Southampton-Winchester road.   But those who care to take the trouble may reach it by a road which extends some two hundred yards or so from the main highway.

The hospice was once described by a very famous archæ-ologist as " first in its class."   It is not only the most ancient charitable institution in the country still functioning usefully, but its rare beauty has been so carefully preserved that there is nothing in England so representative of the best mediæval architecture. Some years after the original foundation, Cardinal Beaufort added to it an almshouse for decayed gentlefolk and called it the " Order of Noble Poverty." Both the benefactions continue to this day and the Brethren

AT ST. CROSS, WINCHESTER.

can be distinguished by their robes. Those of the Hospice wear garments of black, the others wear similar robes of mauve. On the breast they all wear an eight-pointed silver cross, the emblem of the Knights Hospitallers, an order which, during the mediæval period, was devoted to the care of travellers.

To watch them in their picturesque gowns pacing up and down the centuries-old cloisters, or walking in the beautifully laid-out gardens takes one back to other days, and is not unlike looking at an old painting of bygone England.

The church, which is a cruciform structure in various styles, is well worth a visit and the Brethren are always pleased to explain the history of the old place to the wayfarer who is interested.

WASSAILING THE APPLE TREES

The quaint old ceremony of wassailing the apple trees is still observed in many of the cider orchards of Somerset and Herefordshire. This ancient rite takes place on January 17th, the " Twelfth Night " of former days, and even to-day there is a lingering belief in the efficacy of its purpose.

The proceedings differ slightly in various localities, but those at Corhampton, near Minehead, are a good example. This ceremony usually takes place in an orchard three hundred years old, behind the village inn. A special brew of cider is prepared, and on the night of the 17th is carried to the orchard and placed at the foot of the largest tree.

When all the villagers are gathered round the tree the ceremony commences. First, toast, dipped in the cider, is placed in the branches of the tree to get the goodwill of the tree spirits. Then the health of the crop is drunk in cider, some of which is poured over the roots of the trees and the wassail song, a curious old incantation, is sung to the trees by the chief wassail man.

> " Here's to thee, old apple-tree,
>   Whence thou mayest bud, and whence thou mayest
>   blow,
>   And whence thou mayest bear apples enow.
>   Hats full, caps full,
>   Bushel, bushel, sacks full,
>   And my pockets full too, hurrah ! "

When the spell is thoroughly woven and the last words of the toast have died away, a great hubbub breaks out, the villagers whoop and shout, guns are fired through the leafless branches and every possible means of creating

THE VILLAGE SIGN, AND BIDDENDEN CAKE.

noise is employed, so as to drive the Devil and the spirits of evil out of the district.

THE " BIDDENDEN DOLE "

Another very interesting old custom, also dealing with a " dole," is celebrated at Biddenden in Kent. The celebration takes place at 10 a.m. on Easter Monday, at a house called " The White House," close to the church.

It was about the year 1100, so the story records, that two girls were born in the village. Their names were Eliza and Mary Chulkhurst, and they were linked together at hips and shoulders like the Siamese Twins. In this state they lived for thirty-four years. Then one of them became seriously ill and died. The remaining twin survived her sister only six hours, after having resolutely refused to be separated from her by a surgical operation, saying " We came together and we will go together."

They were buried in the Parish Church, where their grave can still be seen. Their memory is perpetuated in the Charity which they endowed by their will. They bequeathed to the churchwardens of the parish and their successors for ever a plot of ground known as the " Bread and Cheese " lands, the rent of which has provided the dole ever since.

There seems little reason to question the main facts of the story, save only the date, which is probably a copying error by some mediæval scribe from 1560.

The " Dole," consists of bread and cheese and " Biddenden Cakes," which are given freely to all comers. The bread and cheese, of course, are intended for the poor, and should be reserved for them, but the cakes are curiosities of the utmost historic interest, and are well worth keeping. They are really more like biscuits in appearance, about four inches in length, and are stamped with a representation of the celebrated twins who founded the dole.

Apart from the interest of the sisters' Charity, the village is well worth visiting. In the main street is a fine old ivy-covered Tudor house, while in North Street, on the side of a building known as Hendon House, is an unusually interesting sundial bearing the date 1626. At the crossroads in the centre of the village can also be seen a handsome " Viliage Sign," bearing an effigy of the Biddenden Maids.

CHAPTER XIV

RHYMES AND JINGLES

Most users of the King's Highway are more or less interested in the old Inns which are found in all parts of the country. Without them, travel would lose half its charm, and wayfarers may well say with Shenstone :

> " Who'er has travelled life's dull round,
> Where'er his stages may have been,
> May sigh to think how oft he found
> The warmest welcome at an Inn."

The old " White Swan " at Henley in Warwickshire, originally built in 1353, claims to be the inn referred to in his poem, which was written at Henley.

While there are many excellent books that deal with the history of our old inns, few contain a collection of the quaint rhymes so often to be found on their signs. I have seen many choice specimens during my wanderings, and pass a few of the best on to you.

On the main road from Newport to Wellington, Shropshire, at the inn called the " Last," this inscription may be read on its sign :

> " All this long day I have sought for good ale,
> And now at the Last I have found it."

Another quaint rhyme from the same district, this time between Wolverhampton and Wellington, was to be found on an inn named " The Beehive," but I believe this has since disappeared. A hive of live bees was placed over the door, with the following lines beneath it, inviting you to enter :

> " Within this hive we're all alive,
> Good liquor makes us funny ;
> Would you one day step in and try
> The flavour of our honey."

A similar sign can still be seen at Grantham. For more than fifty years there has been lodged in a tree outside the inn, a hive of bees ; while connected with the tree and the inn is a swinging sign, which reads :

> " Stop, traveller ! This wondrous sign explore,
> And say, when thou hast viewed it o'er and o'er,
> Grantham, now two rareties are thine,
> A lofty steeple and a living sign."

The inn is naturally called the Beehive, while the steeple referred to is that of the Parish Church, which is a landmark for many miles around.

Other verses, while not actually on signs, are either fastened into the walls or hanging in the bars of some inns, and are well worth noting. One such can be seen on the front of the " King's Arms " at Prestbury, and is of special interest to racing folk. It runs :

> " At this Prestbury inn lived Fred Archer the jockey,
> Who trained upon toast, Cheltenham water and coffee.
> The shoe of his pony hangs up in the bar,
> Where they drink to his prowess from near and from far ;
> But the man in the street passes by without knowledge
> That 'twas here Archer swallowed his earliest porridge."

At the " Plough," at Ford, between Tewkesbury and Stow-on-the-Wold, the following is inscribed on a stone in the wall :

> " Ye weary travellers that pass by
> With dust and scorching sunbeams dry
> Or be he numb'd with snow and frost
> With having these bleak Cotswolds crost,
> Step in and quaff my nut brown ale
> Bright as rubys, mild and stale.
> 'Twill make your lagging trotters dance
> As nimble as the sons of France.
> Then ye will own, ye men of sense,
> That ne'er was better spent sixpence."

GATE INN AT WEST END, WASHBURN VALLEY.

A very novel sign, in the form of a hanging gate with the inscription shown above can be seen at the " Gate Inn," at West End, Washburn Valley, Yorks, and in other places.

The " Plough Inn " at Badbury, near Swindon, has a sign bearing a picture of two horses ploughing. Underneath is the verse :

> " In hope we plow,
> In hope we sow,
> In hope we all are led ;
> And I am here to sell good beer
> In hope to get my bread."

Churches often prove a happy hunting-ground for unusual and rather unexpected notices. Over a church door in Cheshire, for instance, appears the following inscription :

> " THIS IS THE HOUSE OF GOD
> THIS IS THE GATE OF HEAVEN
> *This door is closed in winter months.*"

The last line was probably added at a later date than the original inscription, and suggests rather that warmer climes might be preferred during the cold weather.

Near Dyserth Church, in Flintshire, another notice, the quaint wording of which subsequently caused it to be quoted in more than one of our newspapers, runs as follows :

" No Parking Excepting Cars attending Church Service."

In the belfry of Pitminster Church, Somerset, this quaint notice is exhibited for the benefit of the bellringers :

> " If aney one do ware
> hise hat
> When he is ringing here
> He straite way then
> shall sixpence pay
> In Sider or in Bere."

In the old days bellringing was evidently considered a very thirsty job, for the ringers always had their own pitcher or jack in which to carry refreshments. One such leather jack, which dates from

THE THREE-HANDLED BECCLES JUG.
(1827, Holds 24 Quarts.)

1782 and is to be seen at Lincoln, measures fifteen and three quarter inches in height, while another at Stafford (1750) has a capacity of twenty-seven pints. A pewter flagon preserved at Dorchester (1676) which has on it the inscription :

" To remain for ye use of ye Ringers for ever "

is capable of holding one and a quarter gallons.

Many quaint rhymes can be found on some of the old ringers' jacks and jugs that have fortunately been preserved in our churches. At Great Yarmouth there is one jug dated 1808, which bids you :

" Should you venture up the tower high
To visit ringers, know that they are dry."

The Hadleigh pitcher (1715), besides bearing the names of a number of ringers, counsels :

" If you love me due not lend me
Euse me often, keep me clenely,"

while the three-handled Beccles jug, which holds no less than twenty-four quarts, is inscribed :

" Drink not too much to cloud your knobs,
Lest you forget to make the Bobbs."

Churchyard epitaphs are frequently amusing in their doggerel rhymes. Mark Twain once said of a man that " he could lie like an epitaph," and doubtless the virtues of deceased persons are often exaggerated nowadays ; but a hundred and fifty years ago the truth was told, often with a touch of malicious humour, as, for instance, the epitaph on one John Jackson, to be seen in Dawlish churchyard, Devonshire, which seems to indicate that his relations were by no means blind or over-sensitive as to his faults. It reads as follows :

" Who lies here ? Who do you think ?
Old John Jackson. Make him drink !
Make a dead man drink ! For why ?
When he was alive he was always dry."

Or this epitaph to a man named Chest :

" Here lies at rest, I do protest
  One Chest within another.
The Chest of wood was very good.
Who says so of the other ? "

One of the funniest epitaphs I have found is in Bel-
broughton churchyard, Worcestershire, and may be described
as a very pointed character sketch :

" An honest fellow here is laid,
  His debts in full he always paid.
But what is more strange,
The neighbours tell us,
He brought back borrowed umbrellas."

In a London churchyard there is a monument with the
following quaint inscription : " To the memory of Emma
and Mary Littleboy, the twin children of George and Emma
Littleboy, of H . . . ., who died July 16th, 1783.

Two Littleboys lie here,
Yet, strange to say,
These Littleboys are girls."

A similar example, where play is made on the name of
the person, can be seen at Webley, Yorkshire :

" This tombstone is a milestone ;
Ho, how so ?
Because beneath lies Miles,
Who's
Miles below."

and from Bromsgrove, Worcestershire, comes another :

" Here lies a man that was Knott born,
His father was Knott before him ;
He lived Knott, and did Knott die,
Yet underneath this stone doth lie.
Knott christened,
Knott begot,
And here he lies
And yet was Knott."

The occupation a man pursued is often referred to on
his tombstone, and sometimes gives an opportunity for

some pointed remarks. A celebrated and oft-quoted stone to an innkeeper at Upton-on-Severn bears these words, and there is another with the same inscription at Alvewas, on the Trent near Lichfield :

> " Beneath this stone, in hope of Zion,
> Doth lie the landlord of ' The Lion,'
> Resigned unto the heavenly will,
> His son keeps on the business still."

Blacksmiths' epitaphs are also to be seen in a number of churchyards. There is one at Cheltenham, and others at Melton Mowbray, Blidworth (Notts), Bothwell, Feltham in Essex, Lincoln and Rochdale in Lancashire, to mention but a few. That in Cheltenham Parish churchyard to John Paine, 1796, runs as follows :

> " My sledge and hammer lies reclined,
> My bellows-pipe have lost its wind,
> My forge extinct, my fire's decay'd,
> And in the dust my vice is laid ;
> My coal is spent, my iron's gone,
> My nails are drove, my work is done."

While another in the same churchyard, dated 1825, reads as follows :

> " Here lies John Higgs
> A famous man for killing pigs.
> For killing pigs was his delight
> Both morning, afternoon and night.
> Both heats and colds he did endure
> Which no physician ere could cure.
> His knife is laid his work is done,
> I hope to Heaven his soul is gone."

And in Llanglantwthyl churchyard :

" Under this stone lies Meredith Morgan,
Who blew the bellows of our church organ.
Tobacco he hated, to smoke most unwilling,
Yet never so pleased as when pipes he was filling.
No reflection on him for rude speech could be cast,
Though he made our old organ give many a blast,
No puffer was he, though a capital blower,
He could fill double G, and now lies a note lower."

It is well that epitaphs are not always funny or grotesque.
There are many examples of beautiful and pathetic ones,
such as that which appears on the tombstone of two lovers
and which reads as follows :

" The first deceased ;
He for a little tried
To live without her,
Liked it not and died."

A very beautiful epitaph helps to keep alive the memory
of Sir Philip Sidney :

" England has his body, for she it fed ;
Netherlands his blood, in her defence shed ;
The Heavens have his soul,
The Arts have his fame,
The soldier his grief,
The world his good name."

Another particularly charming one from an old wooden
tablet fixed against the north wall of Crowland Abbey,
commemorating " Mr. Abrm. Buly," his wife and son and
two other children " who dyed in their Enfantry," reads
as follows :

" Man's life is like unto a winter's day,
Some break their fast and so depart away ;
Others stay dinner then depart full fed,
The longest age but sups and goes to bed.
O Reader, then behold and see ;
As we are now so must you be." (1706)

The Litter Lout has been responsible for the penning of several quaint rhymes. For example, near Otford, in Kent, this notice is to be seen :

RESEMBLE *not the slimy snails*
That with their filth record their trails
Let it be said where you have been
You leave the face of nature clean

A LITTER-LOUT NOTICE AT OTFORD, KENT.

Sadly enough, these thoughtless creatures are still only too much in evidence, for one continually meets with overwhelming proof that there are hundreds of such people, who, after all these years of the anti-litter campaigns, cannot appreciate the beauty of the countryside and realise the necessity of keeping it clean. This notice states the case very plainly, and I am sure you will agree that the author of it has certainly drawn a splendid comparison.

Another quaint litter notice, the exact locality of which I have forgotten, was erected on the beach at one of our seaside resorts :

" Who leaves his litter on the sand
    And scatters paper on the land—
May indigestion rack his chest
    And ants invade his pants and vest ! "

I quite agree, and fully sympathise with the authority.
For what mother of a family would be tempted to repeat
her visit to a place where the litter of untidy and thoughtless
visitors was left as a source of danger to her children ?

Another Gentle Reminder to the Litter Fiend, this time
on a notice board at Devil's Bridge, Aberystwyth, reads :

" Ye who pass along these paths,
    I would fain remind you,
Orange peel and paper must
    Not be left behind you.

As we range these sylvan dales,
    Nothing's more unsightly
Than the litter careless folk
    Strew about so lightly.

Whoever sins in this,
    Heedless of these verses,
Surely brings upon himself
    Many bitter curses."

The motorist is another person who has caused many
signs and notices to be erected for his benefit.   One such
notice, a timely reminder on the Cardiff-Newport road, is
given in this queer road sign :

" Life is short—
    Don't make it shorter
By scorching when
    You hadn't oughter."

Another that I have seen in more than one place is also
a " Safety First " warning.   It reads :

" It is better to be twenty minutes late in this world
than twenty years early in the next."

Notice on the Bridge at Halliford.

Rhymes written on wayside direction posts are comparatively rare. Usually, the directions are very much to the
point ; but in the peaceful neighbourhood of Arley and
Great Budworth, in Cheshire, several quaint specimens of
fingerpost rhyming are to be seen, or were to be seen a few
years ago, when the writer was last in that district. Among
others the following caught his eye :

> " Trespassers this notice heed
> Onward you may not proceed
> Unless to Arley Hall you speed."

Another rhyme states that :

> " This road is forbidden to all
> Unless they wend their way to call
> At Mill or Green or Arley Hall."

One fingerpost rhyme that points out a bridle path not
only gives implicit directions to all who wish to travel that
way, but also indicates who shall and who shall not pass
along the path. It reads :

" No cartway save on sufferance here,
    For horse and foot the road is clear
    To Lymm, High Legh, Hoo Green and Mere."

Rowland Egerton Warburton, a fine sportsman who endeavoured during his lifetime to live up to the best traditions of the countryside was the author of these quaint, doggerel verses.

An old notice at Halliford, Shepperton, Middlesex, tells what might happen if you damaged the bridge on which it is fastened :

NOTICE

Middlesex " to wit,"
Any person wilfully INJURING any part of this County Bridge will be guilty of FELONY and upon conviction be liable to be kept in PENAL SERVITUDE FOR LIFE
                                   by the Court,
                    RICHd. NICHOLSON
    24th and 25th Vic. Cap 97.

Bridges in other parts of the country, notably at Dorchester in Dorset, still carry notices to the effect that under an Act of George IV the penalty of vandalism might have been transportation for life.

Not all notices are quite so easy to read and understand as those already mentioned. The one outside a beautiful country inn at East Hendred, Bucks, for instance, appears as shown on page 177. Yet it is not Yiddish, Greek or French, but English. Here is the correct solution :

" Here stop and spend a social
    hour in harmless mirth and fun.
    Let friendship reign, be just and kind
    and evil speak of none."

Another notice, this time displayed in the window of a small village greengrocer, contains quite a geography lesson :

NOTICE

HERESTO PANDS PEN D ASOCI

AL HOU R INHAR M (LES S MIRT)

HA ND FUNLET FRIENDS

HIPRE IGN BE JUSTAN DK

INDAN DEVIL SP EAKOF NO NE

QUAINT NOTICE AT EAST HENDRED, BUCKS.

Apples from Canada and the U.S.A.
Chestnuts from Italy
Dates and Figs from Tunis
Grapes from Bulgaria and Almeria
Grape Fruit from Florida
Lemons from Messina
Melons from Portugal
Oranges from South Africa
Pears from California
Tomatoes from Guernsey
Walnuts from France.

The practice of summing up a county or town in phase or rhyme goes back to mediæval days. Unfortunately, not all the jingles are complimentary, and not all of them are now true, the passing of time having put the rhyme out of date. Here is one from the West Riding which expresses very well the local conditions fifty years ago:

" Bradford for cash,
Halifax for dash,
Wakefield for pride and poverty ;
Huddersfield for show,
Sheffield what's low,
Leeds for dirt and vulgarity."

Another ancient jingle which also states the fame of certain places is this typical Surrey example :

" Sutton for mutton,
Carshalton for beeves,
Epsom for fools,
Ewell for thieves."

A slightly different version, probably written by a Carshalton resident is :

" Sutton for mutton,
Banstead for beeves,
Carshalton for pretty girls
And Mitcham for thieves."

Wayfarers who suffered at the hands of innkeepers in olden days were equally apt at composing rhymes, and that is why, a century ago, a Kentish place-rhyme ran :

" Deal, Dover, and Harwich
The devil gave with his daughter in marriage.
And, by a codicil to his will,
He added Helvoet and the Brill."

Shakespeare is supposed to have given us one of the most concise of these country rhymes.

It was after a drinking match with some of his friends at Bidford, so we are told, that he uttered the celebrated octave of villages, when, " reeling ripe " and having lost the use of his legs but not of his wits, he lay all night under a crab-apple tree. The famous tree has, of course, long ago disappeared, but the spot where it stood is still known as " Shakespeare's Crab." The " lines are quaintly writ " and are as follows :

" I have drunk with Piping Pebworth, Dancing Marston,
　　Haunted Hillborough, Hungry Grafton,
　　Dodging Exhall, Papist Wixford,
　　Beggarly Broom, and Drunken Bidford,
　　And therefore I will drink no more."

Why Pebworth should be " piping " we are not sure,
but possibly its elevation may have accounted for its high
spirits, for, presumably, it was noted for its amateur
musicians. In the Merry England of Elizabeth's days,
Pan still lingered in country places, and the shepherds not
only enlivened their vigils amongst their " silly sheep "
with a " horn and pipe," but often provided the music at
rustic weddings and merrymakings.

Marston, we know, was celebrated for its Morris Dancers
but why Hillborough should gain the reputation of being
haunted is hard to discover, for it is a very small hamlet
with nothing particularly ghostly in its aspect ; but possibly
the bard, as he lay sleeping off the effects of his debauch
under the tree, heard across the meadows " the night owls
screech where mounting larks should sing," and fancied
that " ghosts did shriek and squeal."

From its nickname, " Hungry Grafton," one would
expect to find it occupying " a sterile patch of ground that
hath in it no profit but its name." In reality it is surrounded
by orchards, though it is nevertheless a place where the poet
might easily have failed to secure a breakfast after " a night
out." Exhall is still an awkward place to find and its
rather out-of-the-way situation suggests that the poet,
when bemused by " the hot rebellious liquors in his blood "
found it elusive. Broom is indeed beggarly when compared
with Bidford ; but to call Bidford " drunken " is an
insult, and goes to confirm the condition in which Shakespeare is supposed to have been after his orgy.

One little rhyme which certainly conveys the charms of
the place it depicts is :

　　" King's Sutton is a pretty town
　　　And lies all in a valley.
　　　It has a pretty ring of bells
　　　Besides a bowling alley."

King's Sutton is also mentioned in the following :

　　" Bloxham for length,
　　　Adderbury for strength,
　　　King's Sutton for beauty."

Another quaint jingle which sums up laconically, if not truthfully, the particular features of places, comes from Oxfordshire :

> " Aynhoe on the Hill,
> Clifton in the clay,
> Up to dirty drunken Deddington
> And Kempton Highway."

Farmers and country folk have many hundreds of quaint old rhymes dealing mostly, as might be expected, with their work.

Some years ago, when the barley " mow " was of very great importance in parts of East Anglia, it had a special " health," which was drunk to it, as follows :

> " Here's a health to the barley mow,
> Here's a health to the man
> Who very well can
> Both harrow, plough and sow.
> When it is well sown,
> See it is well mown,
> Both raked and gavell'ed clean*
> And a barn to lay it in.
> Here's a health to the man
> Who very well can
> Both thrash and fan it clean."

Another which is sung at Harvest Home in Norfolk, runs as follows :

> " For all this good feasting, yet art thou not loose,
> Till ploughman thou givest his harvest home goose.
> Though goose go in stubble I pass not for that,
> Let goose have a goose, be she lean, be she fat."

(At Harvest Home a goose was given to those who had not overturned a lead of corn in carrying at Harvest.)

Another quaint old rhyme, this time connected with sheep-shearing, runs :

* " Gavell " = to place in piles.

RHYMES AND JINGLES

" Wife, make us a dinner, spare flesh neither corn,
  Make wafers and cakes, for our sheep must be shorn ;
At sheep shearing, neighbours none other thing crave,
But good cheer and welcome, like neighbours to have."

A comical notice I discovered only last year had been
erected by a farmer in Surrey, who was much troubled
during the nutting season by trespassers in a wood bordering
the roadside, ascertained from a botanical friend the scientific
name of the hazel. Then he put up the following notice
in the wood :

TRESPASSERS TAKE WARNING !
All persons entering this wood do so at their
own risk, for

CORYLUS AVELLANA
abounds here in company with ordinary
ENGLISH SNAKES

The wood was soon given a wide berth by everyone, and
the farmer is now searching for the Latin name of the
common edible mushroom.

Even the poacher can add something to our collection of
rhymes, as I discovered during a holiday in Norfolk, where
I gathered up this verse of an old song :

" As he walked along to work
  And saw his landlord's game
Devour his master's crops,
  He thought it was a shame.
But if the Keeper found on him
  A rabbit or a wire ;
He got it hot, when brought before
  The Parson and the Squire."
        Old Norfolk Poaching Song.

And so on ! There must be many dozens of such rhymes
and jingles which in these matter-of-fact days are dying
out ; and unless they are collected quickly they will pass
from man's knowledge and the lore of the English countryside will be very much the poorer for the loss.

Chapter XV

NATURE NOTES AND ODDMENTS

WAS THAT A STOAT OR A WEASEL?

ONE is so often asked this question that it might be as well to anticipate it.

As a matter of fact they are easily distinguishable, although it would be untrue to say that they are quite different. But to reply merely that a stoat is much larger than a weasel seems worse than useless, because unless you happen to see the two animals side by side at the same moment, you cannot always remember which was the larger. It is equally waste of breath to say that the stoat is paler in colour than the weasel.

There is one feature, however, which can always be relied upon to distinguish the stoat from the weasel. There is no need to remember size or colour, for this one point will answer the question in a moment. If the long, narrow-bodied little beast that comes lolloping across the path when you are strolling through the woods on a summer evening has *a black tip to his tail*, then he is unquestionably a stoat; the weasel has no black tip.

Another simple way is to remember that the stoat in his winter dress is called the ermine, and who can think of ermine without visualising all the little black tails?

THE SEX OF A CATERPILLAR

The proper way of speaking of the sex of a caterpillar is to say that it is " asexual," i.e. without sex, though in it is the potentiality of sex. With the very rare exception of one or two larvæ which are outside the ranks of caterpillars, the larvæ of insects do not breed. It is not until the caterpillar emerges from the chrysalis a perfect moth or butterfly that its sex can be observed.

BERRIES AND WINTER WEATHER

There is an old belief that the presence of a large number of berries on our hedgerows and shrubs is a harbinger of

THE STOAT.

a severe winter, although in some localities one occasionally hears exactly the reverse.

Both ideas are equally incorrect; for while the abundance of berries undoubtedly has much to do with the weather, it is not the slightest value in foretelling the weather for several months ahead. It does, however, remind us that favourable conditions prevailed when the trees were in blossom six months earlier, for it is entirely due to the warm, dry spells during the flowering period that the pollen is enabled to ripen and so make fertilisation complete, thus ensuring a good crop of fruit.

A FOAL'S LONG LEGS

Have you ever noticed what long legs a foal has in comparison to the size of its body? The reason for this is that in the wild state the horse, being an animal of the plains, had to depend upon speed in escaping from foes, and the long legs of the foal are a provision of nature which enables the young animal to keep close to its parents when danger threatens.

THEIR OTHER NAMES

Most wayfarers are familiar with the various names or terms by which horses, cattle, etc., are known during the different stages of growth, or age, or according to the purpose for which they are used. Every child has heard of the names of the different stages in the lives of butterflies and frogs; but there are many other creatures just as well known whose various names for the different periods of their lives are little used except in scientific circles.

The Salmon, for instance, when first hatched, is termed a Parr, and as such remains in the river for two years. During its third year it migrates to the sea and is called a Smolt; it returns to the river again after some fifteen months and is then known as a Grilse. By this time it usually weighs as many pounds as it did ounces when it was a Smolt.

Salmon, as the wayfarer will know, breed in our rivers, and during the breeding season the beautiful steel-blue colour of the male assumes a rather muddy tinge; the fish also develops numerous orange streaks and red spots on its cheeks, which have earned for it the name of the Red-fish. The female at this season also becomes rather darker in colour and is then termed a Black-fish.

There are several other names worth remembering in connection with salmon at various seasons or in various conditions. Clear-fish are fish fit to eat. Foul-fish, are fish about to spawn or just after spawning. Fresh-run fish are salmon which are ascending rivers after having recently left the sea. Kippers are male salmon just after spawning. Shedders are female fish just after spawning. Kelts, or Spent-fish are salmon of either sex returning to the sea after spawning. Well-mended Kelts are fish which, after spawning, have partially recovered their condition in fresh water. Such names, originally local, have become of more general use from having been introduced into acts of parliament dealing with the Salmon-fishing laws.

THE RED DEER

The red deer stag is another animal that is known by various names during his lifetime. Each year, as most wayfarers will know, a stag grows a new pair of antlers, and each year, until he is ten or more years old, he grows on each antler a branch more than he had the previous year. It is from the size and age of his antlers that the stag derives his different names—names now almost forgotten, but household words to the Norman forester, for as the deer grew older so did the sin of deer poaching grow in magnitude.

In its first season, when there are no antlers, the deer is known as a " Fawn "; at the age of about seven months,

MARE AND FOAL.

the first antlers begin to appear, and for the second year, when they form mere " snags " the animal is called a " Pricket " ; when the stag is two years old the antlers develop a small prong at an angle to the upright growth and immediately above the basal collar or " burr," this prong is known as a " brow tine " and the animal is then called a " Brocket " or " Soral." Later a second, or " bez " tine develops, while a third or " trez " tine also makes its appearance. The stag is then spoken of as a " Sore." At five or six years old the antlers are crowned by the " Sur royal " tines, which form a cup or crown and the stag then becomes a " Buck of the first head." As the years pass, points develop on this crown and a stag with three points on each cup is known as a " Royal Stag." With each year new points continue to be added and the massiveness of the antlers, as a whole, increases until the animal is between ten and fourteen years old, when, like those of most of the deer ·tribe, the antlers begin to " go back " or degenerate.

THE ODD PIG

While spending a holiday on a farm, I was much amused to discover that the small pig the farmer's wife was rearing gloried in the name of Anthony, and I asked the good lady why she had chosen such an unusual pet name for the little fellow. She informed me that it was not her choice but it had always been the custom in that part of the country to call the little odd pig of a litter by the name of Anthony.

The origin of this quaint name puzzled me for a long time ; then one day I suddenly remembered having seen and made a note of a pig portrayed in an old glass painting of a saint. That idea gave me the clue, which to me, eventually solved the puzzle. Hunting up my notebooks I found that the saint in the picture was St. Anthony of Padua, a native of Lisbon and friend and companion of St. Francis of Assisi. Like St. Francis he had an especial affection for all animals, and legends say he used to preach to them when men refused to hear him. Because of this he is considered the patron saint of the lower animals, and therefore might be expected to befriend one in especial need of his care, such as the little odd pig of a litter.

All workers on the land love a pig. In the old days the odd pig of a litter—the undersized weakling—was usually given to one of the farm hands for his wife to raise on a bottle. This was a cherished perquisite, and there are over thirty different words still used in various parts of the country to describe it. In Suffolk it is known as a " pignit " or " pitman," in the West Riding of Yorkshire as a wreckling, in Sussex a dolly, in Oxfordshire a dillon, and in Devon and Somerset a cad.

SPEED

Most people, when the speed of anything is mentioned, at once visualise some spectacular achievement performed by a human being with the aid of a powerful machine specially built for the purpose, and are rather surprised to learn that many tiny living creatures perform far more astonishing speeds when flying or running than man, and all in the course of their everyday existence.

It is always a temptation to over-estimate the speed of moving objects, and as many of nature's speedmen appear such tiny things as they go hurtling through the air or over the ground, we are often inclined to credit them with even greater speed than they actually attain. A careful study, however, of some of our birds and animals will soon show that, without the help of a powerful machine, we humans

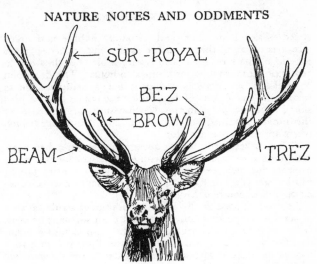

SUR-ROYAL

BEZ

BROW

BEAM

TREZ

A ROYAL STAG.

are mere tortoises. By the police trap method of noting the time required to traverse a well defined distance, it has been found that both the heron and the herring-gull are capable of flying at sixty miles an hour, while on one occasion during the early part of the war I noted that some swifts, that were hawking for insects at an altitude of five to six thousand feet, were easily passing and recircling about my airplane which was registering sixty-eight miles an hour.

Some authorities consider that many birds have two distinct speeds—a normal, for everyday purposes, including migration, and an accelerated speed which is used for pursuit and evasion, in which case double the normal speed is often obtained.

Finches, Blackbirds and Thrushes think little of travelling between twenty and thirty-seven miles an hour, while the noisy old crow, for all his leisurely appearance, can reach thirty-five miles an hour on occasion. Ducks are even faster, but are very deceptive, for they are continually changing height, especially when flying round their feeding grounds. They have, however, been checked at speeds of forty-four to fifty-nine miles per hour.

One of the birds that is often credited with enormous

speed is the Kingfisher, and, although a blue and green streak is often all that is visible as the bird vanishes round a bend of the stream, it is in reality a bit of a slow-coach, rarely doing more than forty miles on hour. The deception of speed is probably caused by the eye being unable to follow the movement of the brilliant plumage as the bird skims over the water in the dazzling sunlight, and also by the rapid movement of the short, rounded wings which often appear as a mere blur.

A few other birds whose speed on the wing has been measured at various times, making allowances for the wind, whether for or against, are : Rooks 24-45 ; Kestrel 35-43 ; Plover 40-51 ; Partridge 40-53 ; Pheasant and Grouse 40-60 miles per hour.

Animals, at least the British ones, are not as a rule capable of such high speeds as our birds, but even so, many of them are great runners. A rabbit, for instance, making for home in a hurry with an ordinary terrier after him, will in a very few yards make it appear as if the dog is almost standing still. I have even seen a rabbit get clean away from a good greyhound. Bunny, of course, knew exactly where he was going, which made some difference, but even then a greyhound is a fast animal.

In comparison to its size, the long-tailed mouse is a wonderfully swift runner, but even they are overtaken and caught by their enemy, the Weasel.

The Stoat also is a swift-moving creature when in pursuit of his quarry, while the Fox, although a good runner, is not extraordinarily fast, and I very much doubt if it could catch a rabbit in fair chase.

The animal that is probably our fastest runner is the Hare. When it really lays itself out to gallop it will often attain thirty to forty miles an hour. Not a tremendous speed, but if compared with that of an expert sprinter it would be seen that man, who makes the most clamour about speed, would be a miserable loser in the race if deprived of his machine.

OUR FASTEST RUNNER—THE HARE.

NATURE NOTES AND ODDMENTS

FLOWERS THAT ATTRACT BUTTERFLIES

Butterflies have a liking for all bright-coloured flowers, but have a special fondness for certain kinds of shrubs and blossoms.

On a Michælmas Daisy plant in full bloom it is not uncommon to see from six to a dozen butterflies; Sweet Scabious, with their honey-laden blossoms, are also often jewelled with these winged gems.

BUTTERFLIES ON PURPLE BUDDLE BUSH.

Even more alluring to these beautiful insects is a shrub from China known as the " Purple Buddle Bush "—Buddleia amplissima, or summer lilac, which, indeed, seems to exercise an almost magical attraction over all the most gorgeous of our larger butterflies. Its lilac-coloured blossoms grow in long, graceful spikes, and they bloom throughout the warm months of the year on a bush that grows in my garden. The common Wild Mint is also a potent lure.

Other showy garden flowers that will attract butterflies are Verbena, Marigold, Lavender and Ivy blossom.

THE STINGING NETTLE

There are probably few people who think of the stinging nettle as being a particularly interesting plant. Indeed, many of us regard it as a great nuisance, especially when it has come lightly in contact with our tender skins. I say " lightly," for there is truth in Aaron Hill's old jingle :

" Tender-handed stroke a nettle, and it stings you for
    your pains ;
Grasp it like a man of mettle, and as soft as silk remains."

But in spite of unpleasant memories, the stinging nettle is really a very interesting plant, and its means of protecting itself are both effective and ingenious. If you examine a leaf or stem of the plant through a good microscope you will discover that it is covered with extremely fine hairs. It will be seen that each hair has a bulbous base from which it tapers to a fine point, where, however, it bends and slightly swells into a knob. At first glance it would appear as though the knob would act in the same way as the button on a fencing foil does, and prevent the hair from piercing our skin ; but the hair just below the knob is exceedingly brittle and the tip snaps off with the slightest touch, thus leaving the unprotected point to do its work.

These hairs are not solid, but are really minute tubes connecting with the bulbous base which contains an irritating corrosive fluid. The slight pressure necessary to push the point of the hair through our skin also causes a tiny drop of the poison to be forced up the tube and into the blood, thus causing the small, white swelling round the puncture, and the irritation.

The reason the sting of the nettle is not effective when the plant is grasped firmly is that the little hairs are smashed and having no sharp points by which to pierce our skin and inject the poison, the fluid simply runs to waste and causes no harm.

So if, during your next wanderings, you happen to be stung by a nettle, try to remember how wonderful the plant really is.

THE STING OF A STINGING NETTLE
GREATLY ENLARGED.

INDEX

INDEX

A LYCH-GATE